KILLING THE SHAMEN

Chief Thomas Fiddler, 1975. Photo, Thomas Lawrence.

Killing The Shamen

Chief Thomas Fiddler
James R. Stevens

Penumbra Press

*This book is dedicated to the memory of
my father, Chief Robert Fiddler, 1860-1940.*

Copyright © Thomas Fiddler, James R. Stevens
and Penumbra Press, 1985, 1986, 1987, 1990, 1991, 1995
(6th printing)

Published by Penumbra Press
Ottawa, Ontario, CANADA
with assistance from The Canada Council,
The Ontario Arts Council, and
The Ontario Heritage Foundation.
Printed in Canada by Coach House Printing Co.

Cover art, Chief Robert Fiddler, 1910
Photo, A. Vernon Thomas

CANADIAN CATALOGUING IN PUBLICATION DATA

Fiddler, Thomas
Killing the shamen

Includes bibliographical references and index.
ISBN 0-920806-81-3

1. Indians of North America--Ontario--History.
2. Trial (Murder)--Manitoba--Norway House.
3. Shamanism--Ontario. I. Stevens, James R., 1940-
II. Title.

E78.M25F53 1985   971.3'00497   C86-003354-6

CONTENTS

ACKNOWLEDGEMENTS

Translations by Edtrip Fiddler, Abel Fiddler, Ennis Fiddler, Tommy Linklater, Sagius Rae and Martin Rae. Special thanks to Shirley Smith and Garyn Wells of the Hudson's Bay Archives, Winnipeg, Manitoba; to Oscar and Jean Lindokken of Deer Lake, Ont.; to Lloyd Bartlett M.D., F.R.S.C., Winnipeg, Manitoba; Tom Faess, Red Lake, Ontario; Fred W. Stevens, Strathroy, Ontario; and Phillip and Helen Doyle, Winnipeg, Manitoba.

PREFACE

IN THE FALL of 1907, one of the most unusual cases in the history of Canadian jurisprudence commenced in Norway House, Manitoba. Charged with murder was old Jack Fiddler, a shaman and leader of the Sucker clan from the upper Severn River in what is now northwestern Ontario. Joseph Fiddler, Jack's younger brother, was also charged. Their alleged crime was the killing of a possessed woman who had turned into the dreaded windigo. The Canadian press emblazoned their headlines with reports of this so-called murder: 'Chief and Medicine Men Choked Out The Evil Spirit'; 'Barbarian Custom Among Indians'; 'Strangler Chief'; 'Devilish Indian Cruelty.' Headlines like these ensured political exposure for all the participants in the trial, especially for the Commissioner of the Royal North West Mounted Police, Aylesworth Bowen Perry. The Commissioner viewed the R.N.W.M.P. as being mainly responsible for Canadian Indians. In the face of a wide range of duties assigned to the Mounties, Perry asserted, 'It does seem that at times the most important reason for the existence of the Force is overlooked. If the Northwest Territories had no Indian population it would need no Mounted Police Force.' The trial of these two shamen would appear to have been a justification of the Mounties' presence in an era when murder trials were a rarity. In 1907 there were only eight convictions for murder among Canada's population of five and one-half million people. Malicious injury to horses (136 convictions) was a far more common crime. It was very unusual, too, for native persons to be involved in any criminal activity. Among the 1,423 people incarcerated in Canadian penetentiaries, only 57 were classified as Indians and half-breeds. In 1907, old

Jack Fiddler and his brother Joseph were the only Indians in Canada charged with murder. The trial, which lasted one day, brought the desired results against 'this savage tribe.' Then the headlines vanished and the Sucker clan of about one hundred and twenty-five natives were forgotten again in their unceded forests in the upper Severn.

What was to remain unnoticed in the public eye would be the duplicity of Aylesworth Bowen Perry and his cruel handling of this case. What would remain unnoticed was the effect this action would have upon the Sucker clan who were involved in a treaty just three years later. What remained unsaid were the qualities of the Sucker leader, Jack Fiddler. The Canadian public had been left with the distinct impression that the shaman had been a banal and devilish person. What also remained away from public scrutiny were several appeals for freedom for Joseph Fiddler who was left languishing in Stony Mountain Penitentiary.

In the summer of 1971, I went to the village of Sandy Lake in the upper Severn River country to meet Chief Thomas Fiddler, the grandson of the shaman Jack Fiddler. From the meetings that followed we began an investigation into deaths that the Commissioner of the Royal North West Mounted Police claimed were murder.

James R. Stevens

PART ONE

PORCUPINE STANDING SIDEWAYS

PORCUPINE STANDING SIDEWAYS

THE SHAMEN, Jack and Joseph Fiddler were the sons of the Sucker clan leader, Porcupine Standing Sideways. The origin of their father is steeped in mysticism. He came as a young man into the forest southwest of Hudson Bay in the late eighteenth century. He was not born into the Sucker clan as a baby; he was a personage who stepped from the other world into this one. It is told that at a longhouse village along the Bay or Severn River, all of a sudden a strange young man was seen standing on the roof of a lodge. He appeared, looking like a person who had just descended from the sky. Astounded clan folk approached him and asked; 'Where did you come from?' The stranger replied, 'They call me the Porcupine Standing Sideways, I lived before in this world, now I am here again.'[1] Records of his direct ancestors do not exist in fur trade journals but his arrival from the other world was prior to 1823; in this year he is listed among the Sandy Lake natives in Hudson's Bay records. He had two wives, three daughters but no sons. His sons, Jack Fiddler, Peter Flett and Joseph Fiddler were born later.

One day, Porcupine would be the leader of the Sucker clan. His name, the clan folk claim, indicate his personal traits were similar to the creature he was named after. The porcupine is a creature who never attacks but retaliates with deadly spears driven deep into the flesh of those who assault him. For all his size, a porcupine can kill the wolf. Porcupine walks in the forest noisily and slowly. He is easily heard. He fears nothing. Yet, when porcupine is attacked, he cries out with the deceptive cry of a small child and it is only the fisher who can kill him. The front paws of porcupine are so much like human

3

hands that many of the Scot traders with the Hudson's Bay Company will not eat his flesh. The women of the clans sew with their mink penis needles porcupine's dyed quills and the magic of their strength into moccasins, gauntlets, and coats. Special respect is given to porcupine. Among the other clans in the forest Porcupine Standing Sideways was well known for his invulnerability and he often declared that 'no person could ever harm me through their spells.' Thus, other shamen were warned, beware of the Porcupine.

The forests that Porcupine came into were poor grounds for survival. For Porcupine's strange birth took place in lands and lakes depleted of creatures. Beaver, caribou, even groundhogs had been extravagantly and wantonly killed in over a century of hunting for the fur trade. Summer hunts and winter hunts left the lands almost empty in the days of Porcupine's youth. No longer did the folk in the clans dress in the long coats of the caribou or in garments of beaver. The fur trade, run with the powerful drug, alcohol, as an incentive for hunting, had reduced the clan folk to a state of destitution. As early as 1804, the fur trader at Osnaburgh House reported that the Sucker clan leader Tinpot's 'whole family nearly starved to death' and to survive had to eat their beaver skins. In 1804-5, fur trader Duncan Cameron wrote a terse assessment of the boreal forest lands, 'the hunt is declining very fast!' Five years later HBC trader James Slater wrote from the Sucker clan's forests: 'As for Beaver skins I have seen none only Cats and few martens and they all make a great complaint theres no Beaver which I suppose to be true or else they would have killed some.' In 1812 near Osnaburgh two brothers and families starved to death in winter! From Moose Lake south of Osnaburgh, George Budge, an HBC servant wrote sadly, 'I never seed starving Indians till this year they are really pityful to see.' Young Porcupine and the Sucker folk were living in hungry times in the headwaters of the Bay River. Here they spent many of their days moving about Windy and Sandy Lake, and Northwind, and Trout Lakes, and Caribou Lake.

Their clan symbol was one of the common fish in the boreal forests. It is a creature that runs up the rivers in prolific

4

numbers after the melting of the snows each spring. The sucker is an excellent swimmer, more powerful in the water, in fact, than many other fish. In the wildest rivers or shallowest streams, suckers swim up rivulets in the forest in a lengthy spawning. Thus, they are easy to catch with one's hands and this fish has saved many a gaunt clansman from starving in the boreal forest. Although these creatures are very boney from their resilient rib cage, the flesh is sweet and oily. In the spring they are harvested in abundance and are a staple in the diet of the clans.

The Sucker in its habitat is tough and powerful and is the symbol of a proud clan which carries its name. Thomas Fiddler explains.

* * *

Thomas Fiddler: Every Indian is related to a creature. This is true of all people. When I travel and meet other people, people from the south, they always ask me who I am related to. In other places there is often someone who is related to the same creature, so is related to me as well. Although this person doesn't know me, he will treat me like a brother because we are related to a common creature.

This is what people ask: 'What creature are you related to?'

One of my friends, Marten, from Cliff Dwellers' Lake met a hunter called Geean, from Red Lake. Both of their clans are Caribou, and once they met they became brothers although they never knew each other until they were mature men.

We teach each other about our clan symbol, the Sucker creature. Now, there is not that much special about the sucker. But, when suckers spawn, even when there is little water – a trickle – a sucker can still climb to the top of the falls. With strong fins it will even go over the tops of steep falls. It's like it flies to get to the top of rivers. So a sucker can go places other fish can't go.

When we get together in a pow-wow, the singers – fish are just like humans – the sucker would sing: 'My fins sound like the roll of thunder when I fly up the waterfalls.'

5

The song comes from sucker flying over the waterfalls.

The clan symbol of an Indian is never changed. Even when women mate, they do not change their symbol. Although a woman is not with her own people and people ask her, they will know where she came from. This is the purpose of the clan symbols.

When a man and woman mate, their children take the clan of their father. Of course there is nothing wrong with people of the same clan getting mated.

* * *

In the 18th and 19th centuries when Porcupine and his kin met with other hunters from different regions they spoke easily and proudly of their clan symbols. When asked to write their names by fur traders, native men draw out the lined form of their clan symbols. On the forest portages, bark etchings are left in view or are carved into the skins of huge trees so people from other clans will know of their presence. Some clansmen have their symbol tattooed on their faces, chests and arms. Above graves, carved in wooden markers, clan signs stand over death. Clan symbols mark shared heritage and differences between the nomadic families of the upland forests.

* * *

There are other clans who wander the upper Bay River forests. THE PELICAN CLAN is named for the magnificent white bird of both sky and water which flies with an eight foot wing span ending in black tips. Pelican has bare orange skin surrounding stunning red eyelids, circling haunting eyes. 'When they rest on the cliffs in moonlight,' it is said, 'you can see lightning flashing in their eyes.' The Pelican clan in Porcupine's days are led by a hunter called 'The Shell.' The Shell and Porcupine are friends, and their groups often travel and camp together and inter-marry.

6

THE STURGEON CLAN is named for the fish which is the largest creature in the lakes and rivers. One fish will nourish a family for many days. Sturgeon is sometimes six feet long and has no scales. Under its broad snout hang four appendages. They are plentiful in early summer when they spawn in the rivers. Sturgeon clan members have many alliances for they inter-marry with Sucker, Pelican, Crane and Caribou clan folk. They are a small group that roams between the Narrows Lake on the Bay River and the east end of Island Lake on the upper reaches of the Thunderbird River.

* * *

THE CARIBOU CLAN is named for that magnificent creature possessing the large spreading rack and a coat that shades into brown and almost black. Caribou has large feet that carry lightly his seven hundred pounds. Caribou feeds on white spongy lichen, lots of mushrooms, shrubbery, and some water plants. The Caribou clan folk frequent Cliff Dwellers' Lake on the upper reaches of Gooseshit River. The Caribou clan folk inter-marry with Sturgeons and Crane members but only rarely with the Suckers.

* * *

THE CRANE CLAN is named for the largest flying creature in the forest. They are ancient brothers of the Sucker clan but they took their clan name from a hunter in the eighteenth century, 'The Little Crane.' This clan is not always on friendly terms with the Suckers and Porcupine. Cranes frequent Cliff Dwellers' Lake and the east end of Sandy Lake.

* * *

All of these clans number no more than three hundred souls. They all live on the edge of extinction for the boreal forest does not have as many creatures it once had for survival. In Porcupine's youth, the forest was without beaver. Long a staple for food, it has been placed on the edge of extinction by over a century of killing it for its fur. At the HBC post on the mouth of the Berens River, a place where the Suckers traded occasionally, the HBC postmaster reported in 1818-19 that his area, 'which was famous for having Beavers and otters formerly-but-at present those Animals is nearly exterminated being long hunted by Different Traders.' At HBC Osnaburgh House the trader declared; 'Scarcely any Beaver indeed I never saw them bring so few and they say that there is hardly any to be found.' In the upper Severn an HBC trader 'found some Indians in a most wretched state and almost starved, being destitute of ammunition, nearly naked and scarcely possessed of a necessary article to enable them to procure a living.'

The difficulty for clan folk to survive when the beaver were exterminated occurred after three decades of extensive hunting. In 1788, 4,200 beaver pelts were collected at HBC Osnaburgh House; thirty-three years later less than 260 pelts came over the store counter. The loss of beaver as a fur trade item was a large factor in the amalgamation of the Northwest Company and the Hudson's Bay Company. Then, all through the boreal forest south of Hudson's Bay, fur trade houses closed up. The Northwest Company post on Windy Lake closed in the spring of 1821 and clan hunters demanded to know why fur trade houses were being deserted, which they represent as being an almost unjustifiable act and ask: "what have they done to be thrown away like dogs?"'

In Sucker territory, however, a post was opened in the fall of 1825 on Windy Lake by the HBC. Within six years the post was shut down again. In 1830, the post reported there was a 'poverty of the country in the larger class of animals.' The folk of the Sucker and Pelican clans took few moose and caribou. In 1832 there was 'the total disappearance of Rabbits all over the District.' In the winter of 1832-33 at Windy Lake 'no less than three whole Families, Men, Women and Children have starved to Death.' Even William MacKay, the HBC postmaster at Windy Lake reported his family were 'obliged to have resource to rock weed for a miserable and scanty meal.' The decline of large creatures, beaver and rabbits spelled death for the people of the Sucker clan; the clan folk in Porcupine's youth struggled to survive. It did not help their plight that the HBC closed their post at Windy Lake in 1833 and moved to Island Lake. There would not be another fur trade post in the upper reaches of the Severn or Bay River in Porcupine's lifetime. This meant, however, that there would be no outside interference in the customs and beliefs of the Sucker and Pelican clans until the early twentieth century. Porcupine would be the last of the Sucker shamen who would not have to answer to the strange laws of the white men.

As Porcupine matured, he became a leader in the harried Sucker clan. His shamanistic abilities, used to protect his people, are recalled in legend.

* * *

Thomas Fiddler: While Porcupine Standing Sideways was living, people could kill each other with their curses. Porcupine is very, very tough but he never bothers anybody without a reason. If a person does anything against him, or his children, then Porcupine will return the same thing to that person.

While Porcupine was living, it was time when people often see windigo in their midst.

At this time there were people coming into the country (Windy Lake) from Lake of White Pine Narrows, Red Lake and sometimes they met the people from Windy Lake. The people from Lake of White Pine Narrows (Lac Seul) were very bad.

All of these people did not have very much, just gunpowder, guns, axes, and matches that they got from the James Bay area. That's how they lived; they didn't even have fish nets.

One summer a man from White Pine Narrows was living near Porcupine and this man went out hunting with his wife and children. Porcupine saw this man come back from the hunting trip and he watched him unload his canoe. Porcupine thought this man had killed a moose and he was hoping this man would give him some moose meat. While Porcupine watched, he saw this man take something out of his canoe that was wrapped up and he thought it was moose meat. But it wasn't meat, it was the body of his child that died while he was out hunting. The man was really mad when he heard that; furious at Porcupine.

At this time there were no nets, and after this incident, Porcupine went out with his young daughter to get some fish from the michikan, a fish weir built below the rapids in one of the rivers. His daughter fell in the michikan and drowned before she could be rescued. Porcupine blamed the White Pine Narrows man for her drowning.

This man had, at this time, returned to White Pine Narrows Lake and he had a weir built on one of the rivers too. This man told his wife to go and see if there was any fish. She took her two daughters with her, one was about sixteen, the other eighteen. All three of them fell into the weir and because it was so cold, they froze in the ice on the river.

In the following summer, Porcupine and his family could not find any food and they were starving. Porcupine blamed this man from White Pine Narrows. By late fall, everyone in Porcupine's village was starving. Their children were so weak they were ready to die. Now, Porcupine knew that all the people from White Pine Narrows Lake were doing this to the people.

All the people from Porcupine's camp got together and said: 'Why don't we call on Porcupine to do something. He is blaming the people from White Pine Narrows for doing this.' They gave Porcupine all kinds of gifts – axes, guns, knives – because something had to be done. All the children were so weak they just lay inside the lodge. After they presented Porcupine with these gifts, he told them to make a moose's leg out of wood and to paint it black with charcoal. Then, Porcupine told the people to clean up the lodge. Everything had to be really clean, even the fireplace. The people did this and they brought in fresh sand for the fireplace.

Then all the people came into the lodge and sat around in a circle. Porcupine lit up long pipe. One man carried the pipe around for everyone to smoke on. Behind this man another man carried the wooden moose leg. After a person smoked, the man with the moose leg asked: 'What part of the moose do you prefer to eat?'

Porcupine had told the people: 'If we can name every part of the moose, then we will get a moose to eat.'

By the time the pipe had passed all the way around the

circle, the people had named every part of the moose. The next morning, Porcupine knew a moose was coming near the village and he asked a man to go out and kill it. By the end of the day, everyone had received the part of the moose they had named. This was the end of the famine; after this they killed lots of game.

Still, the White Pine Narrows man was after Porcupine when he knew he couldn't starve Porcupine's people. The next winter, Porcupine knew something was coming for him. He thought it was a windigo, but it wasn't a windigo. He saw this thing; it was really huge and looked like a bear. It appeared only in the night.

Before the lake froze that winter, Porcupine went down to the shore to get water and he saw this huge Pike. The Pike said to him: 'Why don't you call on me? I promised you one time that I would defend you if you called on me.'

When Porcupine was young, he dreamt about this Pike. When Porcupine was young, he had dreamed and obtained many things on how to defend himself. But all the people from White Pine Narrows knew the things Porcupine depended on for protection. So Porcupine couldn't depend on these things for defence. But Porcupine had forgotten his dream about the Pike and he didn't remember it until the Pike mentioned it to him. Then he remembered the dream right away.

The Pike had said: 'Go out in the bush where you will see a rotten birch tree. The tree will be rotten inside but not the bark. Take away the moss from the birch and put your gun in the hole inside the tree. Whichever direction this creature comes from, find a tree and place your gun there.'

Toward evening – after Porcupine had placed his gun – they heard this creature again. It wasn't far from where they were living. When the creature came close, they heard a gunshot sound. When the shot rang out, they heard a human voice yelling. Porcupine ran out at the sound of this human voice. He saw a little person standing there, yelling. It was a very tiny person. Porcupine told him: 'That's enough. Don't attack me anymore. I'll let you go home now, but the next time I won't let you go home.'

During the next winter, the attack became worse. The man

from White Pine Narrows sent out a windigo instead of listening to what he had been told by Porcupine. Porcupine was up in the Sandy Lake area at this time. It may have been on Narrows Lake.

They used to say that when a windigo was after some victims, people who had power would be drawn into a state when the windigo was nearby. Porcupine and the old men knew something was after them. These old people were lying around the lodge; it looked as if they were dying. Even Porcupine was bedridden. The women and children were alright because it was only the older men who practised their powers.

They could hear a loud thumping in the ground and they knew it was windigo. Every time they heard this sound, they could feel the ground shaking. Eventually, they saw distant flames coming from the windigo creature. The women and children decided to flee because the windigo was so near.

Porcupine's wife had a knife and an axe. When she took a last look inside the lodge, she went in and put the knife in Porcupine's clothing and placed the axe in his hands. Then, all the women and children left and Porcupine got up and went down to the lake to meet this windigo.

When he met this windigo, all of a sudden, the wind started blowing. Clouds formed and trees bent to the ground like blades of grass blowing in the wind. Sounds like shots being fired were heard.

After, it calmed and the women saw Porcupine coming back. He told them the sounds they heard weren't shots. It was his whip. Every time he whipped this windigo it sounded like a shot.

This windigo's hair stood straight up on its head and rabbit fur grew out of its back. Each time Porcupine whipped the windigo, it rubbed its head with its hands to see if its head was still on its body. This windigo was the man from White Pine Narrows Lake that Porcupine had warned, but because he never listened to Porcupine, he was killed right there.

The remains of that windigo were carried away after it was defeated and the people asked Porcupine which one of his protectors had killed the windigo. But Porcupine didn't want to tell them, so he said that it was the spirit of a Sioux Indian that defended him with the whip. But this wasn't true.

They used to say long after this that when the snow is almost gone, just a little of it on the ground, thundering noises can be heard from that place where Porcupine defeated the windigo. The reason is that drops of blood from that windigo were left there.

* * *

A full six years after the starvations among the Sucker, Pelican, Sturgeon and Crane clan in the upper Bay River at Sandy and Windy Lake, the forests are still not abundant with animals. In September of 1839, William MacKay, the HBC trader at Island lake reports in his journal: 'Indians arrived from Sandy Lake quarter have Brought some Furs But Chiefly Musquashes, they also are starving hard.' 'Indians arrived from Sandy Lake Quarter in a pitiful state both cold and hungry and their Garments of Rabbit Skins in a fretful state.' Survival for a native clansman was summed up by the trader: 'The Country is now interly distited for animals, and solely depends upon the Hooke or his Snear when he leaves his Tent.' As for beaver, in 1839-40, the Island Lake post took only 150 pelts in its large district.

Survival in the clans in Porcupine's days meant that young hunters had to gain hunting skills and special powers from the other world. Youth in the clans fast and open their minds while lying alone in the forests for several days at a time.

* * *

Thomas Fiddler: During the winters it is hard for the people to survive. The only way the people know how to survive is through their visions; their minds. So when a boy reaches sixteen winters, his father shows him how to survive. His father teaches him not to bother with girls until after he has a vision.

His father will tell his son to go by himself to a certain place to have visions. This takes place in the spring time when the snow is melting. And when the son goes off for his vision, if he has fooled around with girls, he probably will only learn bad things – visions of evil women and that's all he gets out of his visions. When a boy does not go with girls at this certain age, he will have visions, like trees and animals. He will learn to respect things.

He will learn never just to kill for the fun of it but for the benefit of his people.

He will learn to respect the plants and the trees that give him his tools and his medicines for curing.

He will learn to thank Manitou for his gifts.

To learn this, a son goes out when the ice is thawing. The migrating birds are returning. The leaves are just starting to grow. Parents instruct boys to seek the migrating birds, the winter birds, the animals, the plants in the visions. It is the boys' dreams of these that will help him through life.

* * *

Thomas Linklater: Back when I was a little child, I was taught that you've got to kill a bird. This is when your hunting skills begin. You hunt around to see if you can get close to the birds: to see if you are a good hunter. If you can walk around the bush without scaring anybody, without the birds taking off, you are a good hunter. But we don't kill robins, they are sacred birds. You don't touch robins. Never.

When you kill the first bird, you take it to your godfather – the one who has named you – and give it to him. Your godfather will cook the bird and eat it. This is the first sign of your hunting skills.

The first time you kill a duck, this is important. This first duck you kill, no matter where you are in the bush, you are to smoke it, if you can't bring it home right away. When you get home you give it to your parents. They will prepare a small feast. It is a feast for three or four people: the parents, the young man and the godfather.

Your godfather comes in and he starts saying a few things to you: he explains a few things, what to do in later life when you start killing things. He tells you what to take out of a creature.

Like – when you kill, this is when you know who all the

animals are that you are going to kill – you take a little part out of them. For each animal, take a little part out of it, every time. This you put back in the place where you killed it, whether it's a beaver, muskrat or moose. It's a different part for each animal that must be put back.

When I got my first duck, my godfather came in and told me what I had to do for the animals I am going to kill. For the beaver, right on top of the tail where it goes in the body you cut a little piece out and put it back in the water. You are taught this after you kill your first duck. Your godfather will tell you this and after your parents will keep reminding you to see that it's done.

My grandfather frightened me one time. He said, 'You haven't started thinking about a woman, this is the time for you to go fasting.'

He mentioned things about someone calling to me.

'Three times they are going to call you,' he said, 'don't move when you hear the first person call you. The second time when he calls you don't answer. The third time, that's when you answer.'

'You will be in a state, like a trance,' he said, 'every little thing that moves – like a spider that walks below where you're fasting – it will sound like a moose walking around; like a big monster walking around. It's a weird sound.'

He said, 'Now I'll be there when you're fasting.'

There are four directions where elders put you – north, east, and other directions. When you finish one direction, that is one stage. You finish that and he comes in. You will be sleeping. He will come over and give you some water to drink. Then you change position again. He told me a lot about powers and who would come to visit me.

* * *

Fasting and seeking visions of moose, bears, birds, and fish by youth is an example of the fact that native clansmen in Porcupine's time are 'imbedded in nature.' In the boreal forest: fasting; having a godfather to instruct you; listening to myths; and having parental direction for choice of a mate is a part of clan life. Mating is not a matter of free choice among a people so close to the edge of extinction. The choice of a mate is an important consideration. Alliances between clans result in mutual support and friendship between the folk.

* * *

Thomas Fiddler: The way of the people is different in the forest. The father and mother instruct the child in life and they also decide when, how, where, and to whom children should mate. As the parents bring up a child, they teach the child to obey and honour parents, so when the child becomes of age to be mated, the son or daughter doesn't disagree with the father as to who might be chosen as a wife or husband. Parents decide and try to select a partner who will make a mating that will last through life.

A young man is ready for a woman when he has learned how to hunt and provide and fasted. The young woman is ready when she has learned to clean and skin animals and how to make clothing from the skins.

The father and mother stress strongly that mating should be upheld no matter what the consequences might be.

When it is the time that both a son and a daughter are satisfied with the arrangements that parents have made for them, the parents hold a feast for them. The son's father and mother and the daughter's father and mother gather at the feast. Other people are invited to come and share their joy.

A ceremony is held before the feast begins. The pipe is smoked by all present. They do this to bless the children; to have a lasting bond between them and good fortune in life ahead of them. This is shown by passing the pipe all around the lodging and everyone draws smoke from it. After they smoke, they eat the feast.

At the feast, when these two young people are bound together, it might be the first time they have seen each other.

After they eat, the fathers take turns singing on the drums. When the father begins beating the drum, it is expected the daughter and son will dance: in this way they show Manitou they are thankful they have reached the age of mating.

The father sings over the drum:

'I make all the people happy,
I make all the people happy,
I make all the people happy.

My daughter, you make your new mate happy,
My daughter, you make your new mate happy,
My daughter, you make your new mate happy.

My son, you make your new wife happy,
My son, you make your new wife happy,
My son, you make your new wife happy.'

The father of the son who is getting married gives something important to the girl's father – like a gun. This is done when the daughter's parents agree to the mating. But the son doesn't give anything to his father for making this arrangement.

When I was ready to mate, a woman had already been chosen for me. I wasn't that excited about it. My father had asked the young woman's parents for her: they gave permission right away and she came over to stay in my father's lodging. My parents were living on Windy Lake while this young girl was staying with us.

It was late in the fall, I was paddling my canoe on the lake just before sunset. I saw two moose cows and a calf along the shore. And I killed all three of them. I paddled on back to the camp with the moose. My father and mother took charge of the three moose. I didn't have any say on the moose because I was not mated yet. My father took the fat calf and gave it to the girl's father for a present. This is what I mean: because I wasn't mated my father didn't have to ask me what should be done. I wasn't too happy about this because the other parents got the fat calf.

What often happened, when a parent had a son, two, three, four years old, this parent would arrange with another parent who had a daughter the same age that these two would mate when they came of age.

With mating, the two young people would erect their own lodge and live in the encampment. Mostly, they live in the encampment of the boy's parents.

Sometimes difficulty arose. Maybe the young woman didn't want to mate the man chosen. Still, the young man would just take the woman away with him. Sometimes this worked out, sometimes it didn't.

* * *

It was customary in the lean days of Porcupine's youth for the mature men to mate more than one woman. The leading men at Caribou, Windy and Sandy Lake in Porcupine's youth were Long Legs – he had three wives and twenty-four in his family; Yellow Sky – he had one wife, sevens sons and two daughters; the Tinker had three wives, five sons, and three daughters. Having more than one wife was common and related to the very survival of the people in Porcupine's days. Fur trade records reveal that the clan folk in the Sandy, Windy and Caribou Lake forests numbered only 84 men, women and children in 1823. Nearly 60 percent of this population were women, so numbers alone were a compelling reason for polygamous marriages.

Porcupine, himself, mated in the decade 1810-1820 and was fortunate enough to have, eventually, three sons and two daughters. One son was to gain the English name, Jack Fiddler, the other became known as Peter Flett, the third and youngest was called Joseph Fiddler. All three of these sons were to have tragic endings to their lives. His eldest son, Jack Fiddler was to become leader of the Sucker clan and was, perhaps, the greatest shaman in the boreal forests of the Americas. Shamen in the forest world were both loved and feared, hated and respected. Often duels went on between the shamen in different clans.* Elders from the Sucker, Sturgeon and Caribou clans talk softly about the power of shamen.

*See *Legends From The Forest,* ed. J.R. Stevens, Penumbra Press, 1985.

Thomas Fiddler: There is such a thing as 'amunisookan.' When this happens, people start seeing things – things that are not really there. When people see these things, the shape of them is usually like a human being and they often try to catch it.

Now, I have said that we fasted – went out to try to gain power through visions. Power was needed to get food by hunting the animals. The people try to take care of everything in their lives with this. They realize that Manitou made everything they saw around them. So people that go fasting, gain power, and they come back to try things with their minds. People that used their minds well were good at getting ducks, game and fish.

But some people misused their power on women and evil things. Lots of times these misusers used power against a hunter to prevent him from catching anything. A bad person would do this to starve out a man and his family. When people misuse their power, it catches them. They see things that they try to catch but they can't catch it because it is not a physical thing.

Along the shoreline, the people there don't sleep at night. They run around at night doing all sorts of things. They created a 'half-man' that's what scares them. Lots of people try to catch him but they can't. It's not physical. I tell people not to bother with this because it's not good.

Sometimes it happens that people will finally do something to this thing but they are only doing something to themselves. This little person has the power to make himself seen, which forces the people to do something to him. If a person attacks him, he will only harm himself.

Let me explain. I will tell you a story my father told me.

A long time ago there was a person who bothered everybody. He used his power to cast spells on people. People would hear something but it would not be there. This person was doing this with his mind. But, finally, this person reached the peak of his powers and a spell he cast returned upon him.

It was in the fall. During the night this person started to hear things. The power that was held by some could create visions.

But this person thought that since he had power, there was nothing that could destroy him.

One night this person began to hear thunder. Even the ground began to shake. This happened night after night. The thunder grew louder and louder and came closer to his lodge. It sounded like someone was walking around his lodge. When this thing walked around the lodge, every time it passed the doorway, a wind moved the flap over the entrance. This person wasn't worried. He thought nothing could touch him anyway. He knew that one of the people was doing this to him.

This person finally got angry. When this thing went by the entrance, he ran out with his axe. He saw the thing and he started hitting it on the back with his axe. After he struck the thing several times he went back in his lodge and lay down and was dead. His axe was stuck in his own back.

* * *

I will tell you another story about something a man once did. This man was a relative of Edward Rae. This man was a originally from White Pine Narrows Lake. It all happened on the Long Portage to go to Island Lake. Here people often used to stop to make canoes or repair them with birchbark.

This old man was known to have powers. His name was Ruffy Head. This old man had a lot of daughters. But young men were so afraid of this man that they were afraid to ask for his daughters' hands.

One spring, this Ruffy Head was building a boat. One of the tools he used was a curved knife. He used the knife to peel off strips of bark for his canoe.

People were afraid of this old man and when they killed anything, the usually gave him a share of their kill. One morning one of the people went out to check the net. They caught a few big whitefish in the net. They gave the fish to Ruffy Head. He called his wife and told her to prepare the fish, clean them, and put them in the water until he wanted lunch.

About noon, his wife went for the fish to put them in a pot to boil. She didn't get the fish, the lake waters had taken them away. His wife went up to tell him what happened.

She laughed saying, 'Maybe you give too many orders for preparing your food.'

Ruffy Head was very angry that the whitefish were gone and because of the words of his wife. He didn't like it because of the way she laughed.

All his daughters were across O'pasquiang Lake fetching sucker creatures.

It was a good calm day. The waters were quiet. At almost sunset his daughters were seen coming back on the lake. Where Ruffy Head was standing, there was a small cloud right above him. This small cloud grew larger and larger and soon you could hear thunder in the cloud. The girls were half way across the lake. All of a sudden, wind and rain came down. Ruffy Head and his wife couldn't see out across the lake. Soon they lost sight of the girls.

Ruffy Head's wife came down to where he was working on the birch trees. She asked him to do something because his daughters were going to drown. Ruffy Head was very calm and still where he was sitting although his wife was crying in agony.

His wife grabbed him by the arm and cried; 'Do something!'

He pulled his arm away from his wife and said; 'Laugh – now that something is being carried away on the lake!'

Out on the lake the girls put their paddles over the side to steady the canoe and they were swept safely back to the shore they had come from. When they touched shore, the winds stopped and it became clear again. The girls came across again and got home safely.

All this was created by Ruffy Head to scare the woman for laughing at him in the beginning. That's the end.

* * *

Edward Rae: When a shaman tries to kill another, he uses a marble with a shooter. He will blow that toward that person and even if that person is as far as Sandy Lake, the marble or sharp piece of steel will enter his body. The attacker, sometimes, will just hold a steel hook between his fingers, blow on it, then it disappears.

If the object is not removed from the person it hits then he will be dead in a short time.

When a person knows he has been hit, he has to get it out right away. Another person from around the village, with power, would help him get it out. Now, when someone else is being helped the person with power must be paid for it, so he doesn't waste his strength. When a person with power gives it away or has to use it for his own being – to help himself – the power is wasted.

I have seen many of the items used to attack people: marbles, pebbles, hooks. Deadly things. A person with power uses a lynx bone from the upper hind leg. It is put on the place of penetration; the shaman blows through the bone and the object comes out of the person's body.

One time I saw a man get hit on the leg, near the knee. This man couldn't get it out, so another helped him. He put a plate under his leg, then covered the leg with a blanket. The object dropped out on the plate; it was piece of bone.

When two shamen fight each other with their projectiles, the man with the weakest power will get hit first. If a shaman sends the object back that he is hit with, it will then be three times as powerful; it will be very deadly.

* * *

This is the dark side of the shamen. Shamen with full powers are usually the leaders of their clans because of their ability to cure and heal, to find creatures for food and to ward off attacks by other shamen. In the Sucker clan led by Porcupine attacks by other shamen are rare events. The people are all too busy just surviving. The yearly cycle of life, recreation, and travel in Porcupine's time is thus.

* * *

Thomas Fiddler: Porcupine spent most of his life around Windy Lake, at Caribou Lake, Setting Net Lake, Trout Lakes, at the Sandy Lake narrows and O'pasquiang and Angekum Lake; the reason is that they hunted caribou in this vicinity.

At Angekum Lake there is a big hill and beyond this hill, the land is muskeg. There are herds of caribou there. The muskeg area is where they killed the caribou with flintlock guns. There, they built lodgings of evergreen boughs and covered them with snow.

When they found the herds, they killed a lot off because the caribou do not run away when one is shot. They preserved their meat – pemmican. When pemmican is put in birchbark containers and covered with rendered fat, it will keep for a long time.

In the springtime, Porcupine's people came down the rivers to catch beavers and muskrats. They smoked beaver, muskrats and ducks. These were put in birchbark containers as well. When the lakes were free of ice, they moved up the river to Mud Lake to have their annual Wabino ceremonies. All the people from Sandy Lake, Windy Lake, Cliff Dweller Lake, Caribou Lake and Island Lake gathered there each year to celebrate their survival of another winter. At this time, all the people came to this place, where Porcupine was, because they looked upon him as their leader, the 'wabinowin' of the longhouse.

At the end of May, that's when people start to arrive at Mud Lake. The people stay on the east end of Mud Lake, about one mile inland from the Bay River. That's where they held their ceremonies.

These people know the exact time when the sturgeon will spawn at Cobham Falls, near Mud Lake. They look at the leaves. When they are the size of a beaver's ear, they know the sturgeon will be spawning. Porcupine and the people also knew it was time to meet at Mud Lake by the size of the leaves. The leaves grow very rapidly, in two days they change. It is at this time the Wabino is held.

The Wabino is religious – sacred. The belief is: it isn't good to kill birds and animals just for the fun of it. It's like some people think that one thing is nothing. Manitou doesn't think that way about one thing – that one thing is nothing. He thinks a great deal about it. It is the same way with people, Manitou doesn't think people are nothing, even those that are not good to look at, or are ugly. Manitou does not think that the animals are nothing.

Chief Thomas Fiddler and Counsellor Francis Meekis, 1946.
Photo, Lloyd Bartlett.

All these people, including Porcupine, who practised the Wabino used it because they are thankful for everything they have; even to the rock that lasts forever and the herbs that grow up in the summertime. Because of all these things, they know there is a Manitou and they are thankful.

The Wabinogamick* is built of poles and the entrances are built where the sun comes up and where the sun sets.

At the east entrance of the Wabinogamick is a thick pole called the Wabino atik. The reason for the pole is that it represents a human being on earth. At the base of the pole is a rock. The rock is to represent eternity. There will always be a rock no matter how long other things exists. Even if the world explodes, there's going to be chunks of rock floating around somewhere!

Inside the Wabinogamick, there are two poles at each end that people dance around.

Before the Wabino ceremony starts, it is only Porcupine and the old men who sing and play the drums. At the start of the ceremony, Porcupine will ask his godchildren to open the ceremony by bringing him tobacco and a plate full of food. After the food is eaten, Porcupine starts beating the drums, singing. He tells his godchildren – the children for whom he has dreamed names – to start dancing. Porcupine does this because he is glad his godchildren are healthy and well and he wants them to be happy in dancing. When the godchildren start to dance, the parents are happy. Their children are alive and well.

All the people who have godchildren are sitting in the Wabi-nogamick. When Porcupine finishes drumming and singing, another godfather will drum and sing. His godchildren will join the children already dancing by joining them. Then another godfather will drum and sing. Then the parents join in the dance and after a while relatives join also. Pretty soon, everyone is dancing.

The third part of the Wabino is all the moose hunters who were successful in killing moose. Porcupine, or another leader

*Longhouse Structure

25

like Adam Meekis, the Pelican clan leader, is given tobacco and food and he drums and sings. The moose hunters hold their guns and they dance all kinds of steps. Sometimes, they dance backwards in their joy.

The fourth and sixth parts of the Wabino are a thanksgiving to the fish because Porcupine's people depend a lot on fish. This follows the same pattern as the other parts. A man is picked to lead this as well.

In these days, the men never collect firewood. So the next part of the Wabino is about women; all the women who gather firewood look after the lodges and cook. These women get together and pick and old man to bring food and tobacco to. He beats on the drums and sings and these women get up to dance, carrying their axes with joy.

The next part of the Wabino starts when an old man is given tobacco and arrows by the young boys, from about twelve to seventeen. They don't have many guns and the boys use bows and arrows to hunt small game, like rabbits and partridge. When the old man starts to sing, the boys hold on to their arrows and dance.

The Wabino ceremony comes to an end in about a week. About the day before it ends, they hold a big medicine ceremony. They have a big pot of herbs prepared to keep the people in good health. The people take a couple of sips of this medicine during the ceremony and they will keep the remaining herbs throughout the following winter.

This last day is a big feast for everybody. People bring food to Porcupine and then they sit there and eat it with him. Porcupine takes food around and everyone takes some of it. The food is sacred and the people don't want scavengers or dogs to get at it so all the remains and leftovers are placed up on a scaffold, out of the way.

Just before they finish the ceremony, some of the men prepare a shaking tent. Porcupine goes in there to ask the spirit beings if the ceremony they held is good or bad, or if something is going to happen to the people.

Just before the ceremonial close, Porcupine will close it by beating on the drum and singing. Everybody starts to dance, and even Porcupine, the leader, is beating on the drum and before he goes out he dances around the poles three times and then goes out the east door.

At both ends of the longhouse, men and children pull out both poles and the boulders are carried out. When the inner poles and boulders are taken out they are placed by the Wabino atik pole and left there.

It finishes just before the setting of the sun.

During the summer Porcupine's people roam around the area of Northwind Lake and Windy Lake.

The summers are a time to enjoy life and living. There is Porcupine and son, known as Jack Fiddler, and his sons, Robert, Adam, George Jean Batiste, Charley, Henry, their families; also Peter Flett and Joseph Fiddler and his family; also Adam Meekis and his sons, James Meekis, Joseph, Jake, David, Alexander, Luke, their families; also Sitting In The Sky and the Cranes; also John, Elias and Angus Rae. Then there is Mooniyas, Loon Foot, Mamakeesik and others. They have good times in the summers. Summer is usually an easy time for living.

In the summertime, someone usually kills a groundhog. When they cook it, they cook everything. It is said only the men can eat it. No women can eat it! So, the men go away someplace where the women can't go. But everyone is told where the men are going to eat it, usually near the camp. The men will go and eat it there. All the women are told: 'we men are going to eat the groundhog there.' It is part of a game.

At the place where the men are eating the groundhog, the women attack them. All the women, even the little girls, break into the men's encampment to try and get a piece of the groundhog because they have been told they can't eat it. Old women are on the attack too.

The women try to eat this groundhog. Sometimes, a woman will get a piece of it from a man or the pot. If she gets a piece of it into her mouth she wins. If she can't quite get it into her mouth, the man takes it away, she loses.

Everyone plays in this game, even the old people.

Another summer game is shooting arrows. On the birch

trees, a musky fungus grows. The men in Porcupine's time and before, find an old birch tree with these things hanging on it. They try and shoot arrows through the fungus. They might shoot ten arrows a piece. When they shoot they chant a song: 'Ah-gah-da-no, Bah-gah-da-no. Ah-gah-da-no, Bah-gah-da-no.'

When they can't find the fungus on the birch trees, they use bunches or wrapped pine boughs and shoot at ten bundles with ten arrows. As soon as a man misses, the next man shoots. If a person hits all nine of them and then has one arrow and one bundle left, the last one – tenth bundle – is put on the end of an arrow and moved around so a man can't hit it. But if he hits it, he is the winner.

A time ago, when the people are sitting around the lodge, they play 'Hold the Wind,' a game. They don't have floors in the lodge, only spruce boughs. They have a long stick with notches in it. They place their fingers in the notches and hold their breath then count. A person might go to the top of the stick then start again before he inhales.

In the fall – when the ice has not formed, people move toward Caribou Lake on the river that comes from Owl Lake. There are two falls on this river, they are Cliff Falls and Standing Falls. Between these two falls there is a river and some small islands in it. The whitefish usually come up the river from Caribou Lake but the Standing Falls is impassable by fish. They net these fish.

When they are going after the whitefish, about halfway between these two falls, Porcupine's people block the river off. A large number of big trees are floated down the river and piled to block the stream. They make a fish weir so that whitefish will swim right into it. It is blocked up so that no fish will escape. The fish flow in over the top of the weir and drop in so they can't escape.

When they catch a lot of fish, they dry it and make it into pemmican and they store a lot of fish oil. The gut of pike is blown up so that it is about two feet long. Then fish oil is stored in it. Also, thin layers of whitefish are placed in birchbark containers. These containers are stored out an island, where bark and rocks are placed over them to stop water from seeping in.

At the time of early winter, Porcupine's people make a 'Mis-sayquam,' a large lodge dwelling. It is pretty secure and all the people live in two large lodges.

During the freeze-up, when it is not possible to travel any-where, they usually hold a feast called, 'Wee-kwing-de-na-nong.'

The men, the trappers, gather together in one of the missay-quams.

The Wee-kwing-de-na-nong is a thanksgiving ceremony expressing thanks for Manitou providing for them – asking for strength and to help them have a good winter. That is what the ceremony is all about.

In this ceremony, the men use an empty can and they fill it up with 'weejana,' the sex organs of animals. They make lots of this and they have the ceremonial, praying for this weejana to get animals into their traps. They usually hold a feast, with food that has been stored up and they get out their drums and praise the weejana.

The men have their own cans, and each takes some of this weejana. They use it for bait by rolling up some grass on a stick. Then they dip it into the can and scoop it up and place it where they set their traps.

Women do not take part in this ceremony except as an audi-ence.

When Porcupine is roaming around, he has no idea what Christmas is about. But, he knows that at that time of the year – just before Christmas – the days get shorter; and after Christ-mas, the days get longer.

During this time of the year, Porcupine holds a ceremony. When they have this ceremony, that's when they use their stored food for the feast

After the ceremony, they move toward South Trout Lake, and fish for trout through the ice with hooks. Toward Febru-ary, they move up to Angekum again to hunt caribou.

* * *

For guns, powder, and shot, Porcupine and the clan folk travel to the HBC fur trade posts and use their fur catches for these goods. When the HBC post at Island Lake closed in 1844, the hunters from the upper reaches of Bay River travel downstream to Big Trout Lake to obtain goods. It is at Big Trout Lake that Porcupine Standing Sideways has his name appear in post records in 1848-51. Porcupine's son's Jack Fiddler and Peter Flett travel with him. Then it occurs that Porcupine stops coming down the Bay River from his distant wintering grounds around Windy Lake. The HBC sends Cuthbert Sinclair with a single yorkboat into the western end of Island Lake to re-establish that post in 1864. By 1868, Porcupine and his sons no longer come to Big Trout Lake.

In July, 1868, Porcupine and his sons, Jack Fiddler and Peter Flett, arrive at HBC store in Island Lake. Porcupine takes out 63¼ Made Beaver in trade goods. We see him in the store. He appears not a large man but he shows intense purpose in his selection of goods. He chooses four blankets, five skeins of twine, eight yards of coloured cloth materials, a shaggy buffalo skin, a tin kettle, a white shirt, many files for his tools, two pounds of powder and four of shot, and five pounds of tobacco. For food, he gets one half pound of tea, one and one-half of sugar and one pint of salt. Porcupine, leader of the Sucker clan, does not live off the HBC; he and his family live off the creatures in the forests and lakes of Mother Earth.

Jack Fiddler trades over the new counter in the HBC store on the next daylight. He stands taller than his father and it appears his physical strength now exceeds his father's. Jack Fiddler, like Porcupine, is garbed in pants of cloth and shirts of the trader. Both men wear sashes around their waists and their coats are rabbit skins.

In the store, Jack Fiddler asks to see a flint lock musket. When it is handed to him, he immediately assesses the feel of its weight in his hand. The stock to his shoulder, he tests the pull of the trigger and watches the flash of the flint into the empty pan. He rubs the steel barrel with his rough hands. Nodding yes, the flint lock is taken in trade against the furs he will bring later. Jack Fiddler obtains nothing in food, not even tea. Like his father, he lives from the creatures in the forests and waters of the upland forests.

Jack also acquires an item at the post that speaks about him. He strums and twangs a jews harp between his lips and he quickly decided to take it. He has a larger interest, however, in another musical instrument that he sees at the fur trade posts. For this interest, he receives his English name.

* * *

Thomas Fiddler: In the early days, the Indians only had one name, their Indian name. Even Jack Fiddler: the people do not call him Jack Fiddler. Our people call him, He Who Stands in The Southern Sky.

Now, He Who Stands in The Southern Sky and all his sons can play the fiddle – even my brothers played it – and when the white men came, they saw they could all play the fiddle. So, they call them: 'Fiddlers.'

Jack and his sons saw the fiddle instrument somewhere. They tried to make one from a long handled pan by putting a little stick across the handle and then put strings of sinew on it. After this, they switched to wood and made them exactly the way they look now; they carved them out of birch trees.

They made homemade bows out of sturgeon guts. It is taken out and boiled, then it gets hard; just like the wood bows now. They learned to make a lot of things by themselves in those days.

Jack and his sons started dancing to the fiddle. But, at this time, they did not have any houses where they could dance. On a flat rock island on Caribou Lake – it was like a floor – and this is where they usually held dances. They danced on the island nearly all night.

The name Fiddler is used in 1906 but it started before that, when Robert Fiddler was a young man. It was when they started trading that we got two names.

* * *

In the 1880s, the winters pass through summers into snows again and again, the Sucker clansmen return constantly to HBC Island Lake. Jack Fiddler, Peter Flett, and Joseph Fiddler, sons of old Porcupine, come to Island Lake while Porcupine stays back at the Windy Lake forests. Porcupine is way too old to travel. Other hunters come to Island Lake as well. The Meekis of the Pelican clan, the Mamakeesik and Raes of the Sturgeon clan, the Linklaters of clan Caribou and the Cranes led by Sitting in The Sky. All these hunters, many now with English names, now will face times of trial. The winter sweeps the forests from 1890-94, leaving the lands barren and freezing in whiteness. During the long snow days evil other-than-humans appear. Creatures disappear and windigo, the cannibal, often roams. There are stories of windigo circulating.

* * *

Edward Rae: I heard this story from my father, John Rae. It was about one person turning into a Windigo. They used to go trapping and this person went with his wife and four kids. Toward winter, he used to come back to the main camp, but this winter, the man never came back.

An old man at the main camp knew something was wrong; he used to tell his wife this trapper would do something if he didn't get home by dark each day.

The man on the trap line never stayed out after dark.

One time, the man never came back and it was getting dark. When he came back after dark, there was something wrong with him. He killed his wife and four kids and started eating them.

This old man, John Doggy*, knew there was something wrong because the trapper should have been back at the main camp. John Doggy knew a man at the HBC who had power and he asked this man to go with him to check on this trapper.

They went to the HBC store to ask for three items; chains, strong rope and two strong tarps, to take along when they checked this trapper. They left: John Doggy knew where his trap line was.

They used a dog team, five of the strongest dogs and the biggest toboggan they had. As they got nearer the trapper's camp, they knew the trapper was coming back to Berens River so

*John Doggy alias John Thomas was a half-breed who worked for the HBC at Norway House and Berens River.

they made a fire where they could watch him coming.

When they made a fire, they put spruce boughs on both sides of the fire. Then, they sat there waiting and watching. As they were waiting, they saw him come out of the bush and he had his pail in his hand. As the trapper was coming closer they had the chains and rope ready – the tarps were on the toboggan.

John Doggy told the other: 'I will jump him and have the rope ready.'

As the trapper got to the fire, John Doggy told the trapper to sit on the other side of the fire. When the trapper settled down, John Doggy jumped over the fire and grabbed the trapper.

The other partner gave him the rope and they bound the trapper hand and foot. After they tied him up, the trapper started growling and he grew larger and larger. There was a noise coming from the trapper that sounded like pieces of ice grinding together. Then they used the chains to tie him up.

Then they tied him on the toboggan, they used the tarps to keep him tied on. After they finished tying him up, they looked in the pail the trapper was carrying; it contained two small feet of his child. It was an extra meal for the journey back to the main camp.

Then they headed for the main camp and they travelled all night until they reached it.

Back at the main camp, they took the Windigo to a white man's lodge. John Doggy kept the Windigo there because he was the only one who could over-power the Windigo.

After the Windigo was settled in the lodge, the white people gave the Windigo some whisky. The Windigo stayed in the lodge for one day. Then they hauled the Windigo with horses and a sleigh across Lake Winnipeg. John Doggy stayed with him all the time. They took him to Poplar River and they gave the Windigo a lot more fire-water than before.

When the Windigo woke up, they asked him about his wife and kids. The Windigo replied: 'They are still living. No. I killed them.'

Then the Windigo started crying.

After a while, they took the Windigo farther and put him on the train. John Doggy was still along. They took the Windigo to a mental hospital and gave him firewater and shots to

Alfred Fiddler, 1947. Photo, Lloyd Bartlett.

control him. In the mental hospital the Windigo woke up for longer periods of time. He asked for his wife and children. Then he said: 'I believe I killed my wife and child.' Then he started crying. He would stay awake for three hours but he would be crying all the time. The hospital thought he was getting better but he cried all the time.

Soon after, when the Windigo's mind was clear, he was still always crying. He was sure he killed his wife and kids. He had treatment but, eventually, he just died. John Doggy stayed there until the man died, then he went home.

I saw and knew John Doggy. He was an old man when I saw him. He lived at Berens River. When that Windigo got big, John Doggy would slap him and tell him he would kill him if he didn't stop growing big.

* * *

Windigo is a dangerous and threatening reality in the clan folk's comprehension of their boreal forest. For those raised outside the forest the windigo fact was difficult to accept. William 'Big Bill' Campbell, the HBC postmaster at Island Lake became upset when one of the young hunters who traded with him was shot as windigo at Sea Gull Bay on the south side of Island Lake. He reported this death to his superior, J.K. McDonald, who was also a magistrate at HBC Norway House. He, in turn, reported the death to the Lieutenant-Governor of the District of Keewatin. Lieutenant-Governor Schultz's response was, 'That while he regretted to hear of the murder he hoped there would not be any expense incurred in connection with it.' Campbell then stated he would no longer take any interest in Windigo deaths as the Lieutenant-Governor, 'would not act.'[2] Campbell decided he would have to accept the fact that windigo existed in the forests. The fur trade was what counted.

In the fall of 1891, William Campbell becomes alarmed about the Sucker hunter's trade accounts. No one from Porcupine's Sucker clan came to Island Lake in the early part of the winter. He decided to find the reason for not a single hunter's appearance from the distant Windy and Caribou Lake country. On the 7th, he sends out two of his outpost

35

runners, his father-in-law, David Munro, and John Mason, an Island Lake hunter to find old Porcupine's Sucker camp. Later, under a bleak February moon, the two dog sledders return with very few furs to tell that:

'Jack Fiddler having gone into Grand Rapids with their hunts in the first part of the winter which accounts for their not hunting now. They are all heavily debted and there is very little hopes of their paying their debts as they used to make the bulk of their hunts in the first winter.'[3]

A few days later, Jack Fiddler's oldest son, Robert, with Enos Loonfoot, snowshoed to the Island Lake post for supplies. They 'brought nothing,' Campbell writes in his journal, 'their Band has been sick all fall and, therefore, not hunting according to their Account.' A spell of sickness has fallen among the people and men have little strength.

Near the end of March, Campbell sends off James Kirkness with ammunition for the men of Jack Fiddler's camp. On April Fool's day James is back at Island Lake. 'The Cranes' James says, 'are doing very little' and Jack Fiddler's 'have no furs at all because they are starving and cannot hunt.'[4]

After the long winter finally melts away, Sitting in The Sky and the Cranes, who hunt at the eastern reaches of Sandy Lake, come into Island Lake with their spring hunt. They bring 'quite a few Bears and Musquash but a great decrease in other furs.' Next day, Jack Fiddler and old Porcupine's Sucker men arrive at the post. When Campbell opens their fur he discovers they bring 'nothing but Musquash.' He supplies them with nothing but a little tea and tobacco. When the sun brightens the next morning, the Suckers and Cranes leave the post in thirteen birchbark canoes.

In late August, 1891, the yorkboats from Norway House with another year's supplies arrive at Island Lake. All the families around Island Lake and the upper Bay River come again to the post to take debt for furs. There are at least twenty canoes beached below the post and over sixty hunters waiting to see the new shipment of goods. But, the previous winter has given up few furs to pay debts.

36

'I am "giving out," Campbell says, "very little debts some men not even supplied with necessaries for hunting as their hunts last winter did not come to more than a few find skins MB. Some of the Indians started out today as they are starving – having nothing to eat." '[5]

Now, Jack Fiddler and sons, Robert, Adam, George, Jean Batiste, Ennis, Charley, numbering thirty odd, and his aged father, Porcupine, face another winter with little to sustain them. Soon, there is more than suffering among people. Early in the winter, a group of grim men from the different families walk out of the Bay River country with furs. Debt must be held by sadness – are Peter Flett and Papaquatem of the Crane clan, David Meekis of the Pelican clan, and George Fiddler from the Sucker clan. They tell Campbell of their trials and at night he writes in his post journal.

'They report the Bands are doing very poorly in the hunting kill owing to Sickness. They also report 6 Deaths one Pemicheka* (120 years) the Chiefs Father one woman and 4 children. Each of Miscenaweninews** Band have hunted a hundred Rats each some of the Cranes have 10 MB each they got nothing.'[6]

Peter Flett of the Suckers, David Meekis of the Pelican clan, George Fiddler of the Suckers and the Crane get nothing from the post. They have travelled out eight nights on the winter trails to pay off a past debt with muskrats. Six of their people are gone from living, including the old clan leader, Porcupine who, it was reported, lived over a century. They snowshoe back to their winter camps, their food sacks empty. Now, Jack Fiddler, known to the people as, He Who Stands In The Southern Sky, is the clan leader of the Sucker people. He, like his father, lives in lean times.

*Porcupine Standing Sideways
**Jack Fiddler

PART TWO

JACK FIDDLER

JACK FIDDLER

Jack Fiddler could kill a windigo

WHEN SUCKER CLAN leader, Porcupine, passed beyond in the desolate fall of 1891, his son, Jack Fiddler, could count at least sixty winters. This fiddler-playing clansman of the Suckers became clan leader. There was no ritual installation for Jack Fiddler. He became clan leader by virtue of inheritance and his astonishing visionary ability that gave him an awesome reputation for curing, and relating to the creatures of the forest. There was little reason for clan people to be anxious about his capabilities. He had been up and down the forest rivers in his youth. From York Factory in the northwest to Big Trout Lake and Fort Severn in the northeast to Little Grand and Berens River to the southwest; Jack Fiddler knew the reaches of the boreal forest.

Fiddler's direct influence extended to the 100-120 people of the Sucker and allied clans on the isolated branches of the upper Bay River. He also had some influence with Sucker clansmen who lived over the long portage from the Bay River to the upper lakes of the Thunderbird River at Island Lake and Red Sucker Lake.

Clans beyond the Bay River system knew his reputation, and the Loons and Kingfisher clans to the southwest, along the Berens River, were fearful of even entering Sucker forests. These clans in the southwest viewed all the hunters of the upper Bay River as Sucker people. This was not the case. But other clans, with the exception of the Crane clan led by Sitting In The Sky on the upper end of Gooseshit River, and another Crane clan on east Big Sandy, were allied and inter-married with the Suckers.

Clan alliances to the Suckers are evident in the marriages of

41

Jack Fiddler's sons and daughters from his five wives.

Jack Fiddler's wives were: Kakakwesic; Nakwasasive; Nocome: Kaopasanakitiyat; Kayakatopicicikec; (Clans Unknown). His Wives' Children were:

Robert Fiddler	*mated*	Elizabeth Mooniyas *Sturgeon clan*
	mated	Elizabeth Loonfoot *Sucker clan*
George Fiddler	*mated*	Nancy Mamakeesik *Sturgeon clan*
Edith Fiddler	*mated*	Alfred Meekis *Pelican clan*
Nancy Fiddler	*mated*	Angus Rae *Sturgeon clan*
Paul Fiddler*	*mated*	Jemima Wood *Island Lake, clan unknown*
Mary Fiddler	*mated*	John Rae *Sturgeon clan*
Jessie Fiddler	*mated*	Tommy Wood *Island Lake, clan unknown*
Adam Fiddler	*mated*	Eva Meekis *Pelican clan*
Bella Fiddler	*mated*	Moses Mamakeesik *Sturgeon clan*
Betsy Fiddler	*mated*	Sandy Mamakeesic *Sturgeon clan*
Jean Baptist Fiddler	*mated*	Emma Mamakeesic *Sturgeon clan*
Ennis Fiddler**	*mated*	Nancy *clan unknown*
Edward Fiddler**	*mated*	Ellen Beardy *Sucker clan*
Charles Fiddler	*mated*	Martha Kakekagamic *Crane clan*

Jack Fiddler's younger brother was given the name Peter Flett by the fur traders at Island Lake. Among the clans he was known as Across The Sky Man. Peter Flett had two sons, Edward and Andrew Flett. Jack Fiddler's youngest brother, Joseph had two wives: Charlotte Mamakeesic (Sturgeon clan) and Second woman (clan unknown). His wives' children were:

Tommy Fiddler*	*mated*	Wasapeekway *clan unknown*
Thompson Quill	*mated*	Meekis Woman *Pelican clan*

Joseph also had two daughters but it is not recalled who they married.

The Pelican clan who roamed the Caribou Lake area were long allies of the Sucker people. Both clans shared the forest territory at the upper end of the Bay River and their camps could often be found together. The Pelican clan in 1885-86

* Paul Fiddler settled at Island Lake.
**Both Ennis and Edward Fiddler settled at Fishweir Lake.

was listed in terms of its hunters in Tom Linklater's HBC Island Lake Journal.

Adam Meekis (Long Fellow)

1st son	2nd son	3rd son	4th son
Joseph Meekis	James Meekis	David Meekis	Alexander Meekis
(Skapawish)	(Wasakooweas)	(Katowatum)	(Toweass)

The other families associated with Jack Fiddler's Sucker clan besides those in the Pelican and Sturgeon clans were the families who were named in English; Loonfoot, Mason and Mooniyas. Against the Royal North West Mounted Police, it appeared that Jack Fiddler had only forty men to defend his forest grounds.

The leader of the Crane clan, Sitting In The Sky, led people that were also a composite of clans. These people were Cranes, Caribou and Sturgeon clansmen in association. They were on strained terms with the Suckers led by Jack Fiddler. But there wasn't any open conflict between the Crane and Sucker leaders and occasionally there was co-operation and sharing. It was a matter of competition and reputation between two powerful clan leaders that led to tensions between the two groups. Had Sitting In The Sky and Jack Fiddler formed a oneness for defense, they would have raised only sixty-five men.

A second Crane clan in the upper Bay River hunted and fished at the east end of Sandy Lake. This group was led by Kakekugamik and Kakekapetum and they are said to have come up the Bay River from the east. These Crane people, living some 100 miles by water from the Cranes of Sitting In The Sky and 200 miles from the Sucker and Pelican Clans, were too distant to be involved with Jack Fiddler's people. They were the smallest of the three clan groupings numbering no more than fifteen hunters.

Legends about Jack Fiddler recall his uncanny ability to communicate with forest creatures and his duel with windigo.

*This Tommy Fiddler (d1920) was the namesake of Thomas Fiddler, son of Robert Fiddler.

During his long life he said that he destroyed fourteen windigos. So, among his clan, he is a challenger of evil forces and a curer of the ill. He is also a prophet and in his dreams he communicates with creatures who supply the sustenance for his Sucker clan people.

When the Cree Methodist missionary, Reverend Edward Paupanakiss, of Norway House, talked to Jack Fiddler at Island Lake about the benefits of Christianity, Jack, strong in his own beliefs, told him:

> 'I believe in my dreams. Everything we dream is right for us; by our dreams and singing and conjuring in the shaking tent we can see meat, moose and deer for us. Our dreams are our religions.'

Jack Fiddler, nevertheless, once tried to appeal to Jesus for his needs. Thomas explains:

* * *

Thomas Fiddler: When the first minister came in, he told Jack Fiddler that when you asked the Lord for something, you got it. When this first minister tried to teach the people to pray, Jack was told to ask the Lord for whatever he wanted; good health and all sorts of things. That evening Jack told everyone in the lodge that he was going to pray and everyone was to be quiet. Everyone was tense, they didn't know what would happen.

Jack said: 'Lord, I want you to give me a little spoon because I need it to mix my medicine.'

Jack said: 'Lord, I want you to give me a file because I have nothing to sharpen my tools with.'

Nothing happened. Nothing whatsoever happened. That was not good enough for Jack Fiddler.

* * *

So Jack Fiddler, in 1892, was a leader who had full faith in his roots and he stands, in forest stature, as one of the last native leaders maintaining his clan's freedom in Canada. In the west,

Big Bear, Crowfoot, Poundmaker; the half breeds, Riel and Dumont, had all been crushed by the forces of the Canadian government. Jack Fiddler and the Sucker clan in the upper reaches of the Bay River had been by-passed by the main stream of European settlement. But Jack Fiddler, from his visionary dreams, knew that strange machines would be coming. He also foresaw that an injustice was going to occur. Our Sturgeon elder from Caribou Lake tells two stories.

* * *

Edward Rae: When Jack Fiddler went for his dreams, he travelled up through ten different worlds. There were ten different kinds of people in these worlds and that includes this world. Jack also dreamed that there were ten different worlds underground. Jack dreamed about machinery as well and he said that at first, the white men would have these things, then the Indians would have them. He also dreamt that there was a box flying around, and that he came out of his box.

I heard many times that while Jack Fiddler was beating his drum and singing, he knew that airplanes will be coming to help the people. Jack sings about airplanes will be coming to help the people. Jack sings about airplanes and their existence long before anyone saw them.

While he was singing and beating his drum, he chanted

From the flying box I get out.
From the flying box I get out.
From the flying box I get out.

* * *

This is a story that Jack Fiddler told his people. I learned this story from Jack's son, Adam Fiddler.

A couple of men were living in this camp and one of these men killed a human being. One of the men had not taken part in the murder but both men were arrested by the police. They were taken to court, both were charged with murder. Both were condemned to die.

45

These two men were ordered to stand in the same place. They had heavy chains tied around their ankles and there were chains around their necks. The neck chains were made so they would not cut into their necks when they died.

The first man to be killed was the man who was innocent. A minister was called to pray for the first man.

'What is your prayer?' the minister asked the man.

The Indian said: 'My prayer is to get to Kichi Manitou because I am dying by mistake. I am giving my life away, so I want to reach Kichi Manitou.'

The place where this man was standing with the chains around his ankles and neck – they dropped him in that place and he stretched out and died.

The second man, the murderer, was put in the same place as the first man who had been killed. He was on the same platform. The chains on his body weighed about one hundred pounds each. They rolled these heavy steel balls off the platform to stretch this murderer out. But the chains just broke off his ankles and the man just stood there. He never moved. The executioners tried this three times and three times the chains broke off his ankles.

The executioners decided to try and kill him another way. They took the man to a metal pole that had steel needles – like sharp nails – coming out of it. A metal cable was attached to the Indian's neck. They were going to pull him up the side of the pole. When they pulled the cable to haul the man up, it broke. Three times they tried to haul this man up, and each time the cable tightened from slack, and broke.

They brought out a cannon and loaded it. They tried to shoot the murderer three times but each time the cannon would not fire. Next, they tried to stab the man with a long sword but each time the sword touched his body, it shattered. Then they bound the man, hand and foot, and placed him in a coffin. They nailed the lid down tight on the coffin and took a saw and tried to cut the coffin in half. Three times the executioner tried to saw the man in half, each time they failed.

When they took the man out of the coffin, a sound was suddenly heard booming away up in the sky. At the sound, a piece of paper floated down to earth and it landed beside the police who were trying to kill this man. On the paper was a picture of Kichi Manitou along with the man who had been executed. The police were frightened when they saw this paper. The leader of the police was frightened too.

The police asked this man what he wanted. 'Riches. A house. Anything you want, we will give you.'

The man said: 'I don't want your money or a house. Nothing. I want you to take me home, where you brought me from, and leave me there.'

When they took the man home, they asked the man again, 'Don't you want something, a net, some traps, snare cord?'

The man said, 'I don't want anything.'

The reason this man could not be killed was that he had lived a good life. He was not at fault. It was the man who had died first that was the murderer.

This is what my grandfather, Jack Fiddler, said about the protective powers of Kichi Manitou. Jack had such protection; that's how he lived through so much danger.

* * *

Jack Fiddler's position as Sucker clan leader did not just rest on his prophecies – or his ability to tell stories. Story telling and family history were part of any elder person's role. More important was Jack Fiddler's curing skills and his ability to call creatures for people's needs. This made Jack's reputation for the shaman who could cure with his herbs and tell the people where food was in times of need. He was an effective leader.

* * *

Thomas Fiddler: People do not understand about the word 'chief.' The reason Jack Fiddler is a great man is that he can make Indian medicine to heal the sick. People from close-by settlements heard about his healings. When the people heard this, they began to look upon him as the leader, the ogema, but he is not a 'chief.'

Now I will tell you about Jack – He Who Walks In The Southern Sky.

There is a certain place around Trout Lake called Rathouse

47

Creek. It is a high creek and when you look down you see a boulder shape along the shore. The creek winds around and when one comes to the end of it, and you look, you will see a sort of hill: a very big rock. This is the place Jack Fiddler used to get herbs from.

The only time my grandfather got those herbs was in the spring, when this stream had thawed out but the lakes were still frozen. There used to be a lot of muskrats at sunset; they heard the sound of a drum noise coming from the bottom of the stream. Sometimes is sounded like the drum noise was right on the surface. When this happened at sunset – the stream open but the lakes still frozen – Jack Fiddler went into the rock and visited the Cliff Dweller and collected herbs there. He does this once a year, every spring.

The herb medicine Jack gets is put in a little bottle.

One time Bella Linklater – before she was married – and Ellen Meekis, Big Trap's wife and Big Mary Rae had facial problems. Something was wrong with their heads; their faces were very distorted. It is called pee-mee-quay-skat.

Jack Fiddler got three oval rocks and heated them up in a fire. Then he got a bowl, put moss in the bottom of it and put the three rocks in it. He pounded his medicine into a powder and sprinkled it on the rocks. Next, Jack put a blanket over the women and they breathed the smoke coming of those red hot rocks. Those women inhaled the fumes and they sweated a lot but soon their distorted faces were normal again.

* * *

I will tell you another story about the power of Jack Fiddler's medicines. A long time ago the whitefish in South Trout Lake were infected with worms and they could not be eaten by the people. My grandfather, Jack Fiddler, got into a canoe and paddled out in that lake. On the lake, he took out a long pipe. The pipe was lit. He puffed on it as he turned the canoe around in a circle on the lake. After he finished smoking, he went around the lake and dropped his medicine in the water. My grandfather cured the whitefish in that lake. After this, the whitefish were fat and juicy and they did not have worms.

* * *

This is also a story about my grandfather, Jack Fiddler talking – in his mind – with a creature.

There is a certain falls that is not far from here, Cobham Falls, near the Manitoba border. The sturgeon below the falls had already spawned. Jack did something about those falls to make them come back.

This event with the sturgeon happened during the spring-time, a long time ago, when the Indians used to have the ceremony, the wabino-gamick; people used to come from all over the place to go to that ceremony at Mud Lake. Before the falls, a river runs out of this small Mud Lake. It was all along the shores of this river the people used to camp. After the ceremony, they went up to the falls to catch the sturgeon.

They used a net, a big net, a sort of sack-shaped thing. They used lots of boats to drag the net through the water.

But, one time, when they had that particular ceremony, they came to the falls and the sturgeon had already gone. There were lots and lots of people from all over the place. All those people said they should give something to Jack to make the sturgeon come back. They gave Jack clothes, tobacco and tools.

Adam Fiddler was a young man, and Jack asked him and his other son, George, to go with him to the falls.

When they got close to the falls only Jack and Adam went. George stayed with the canoe. The first little ripple in the river was about four miles from the falls, and they walked to the other side of the falls. There were rapids between the first rip-ple and the falls so they couldn't go that way, they might scare some sturgeon. So, they followed the side of the river.

Adam Fiddler didn't know everything his father took with him. He took – you know the rabbit in the winter time when it is all white – he took the head of that rabbit with him. Jack had a pole with him about six feet long. He peeled the bark off it, and put the rabbit head on the end of the pole and he put it down near the top of the falls where the water went over. The rabbit head looked down the river.

After that Jack and Adam just went home. They went down

49

past the ripple to a large pool in the river. Jack put more medicine in the water there. After, they went home by canoe.

The next morning, Jack told Adam and George to go and look where he sprinkled the medicine. They were to beach the canoe in the same place as before and to look in the pool. They had to walk from the canoe and not go close to the river, they could see sturgeons sticking their heads up all over the place.

The next morning, the people went over to the base of the falls where the sturgeons were trying to go. They took Jack along when they went for the sturgeon. That morning, they killed lots of sturgeon. After they got all the sturgeon out, Jack said there was still one left – the leader of all the sturgeon. About ten canoes went for that sturgeon; they were birchbark canoes. They had a hard time hauling that sturgeon in – it was almost the size of a canoe – because it was swimming the other way. All ten canoes finally dragged it to the shore.

Then the people went back to the wabino ceremony; they had a lot of food and were very happy.

* * *

Another ability was vital for a strong leader in the clans. Few men had it: the strength and fortitude to ward off death and attack from Windigo. To the clans, Windigo was satanic and universally feared in the forest. For Windigo was a human possessed with cannibalism and a voice so evil that its sound paralyzed human beings.

* * *

Edward Rae: Jack Fiddler could kill a windigo. The reason he had such powers – to kill a windigo – is because he slept and dreamed. During these dreams, he was given the power to kill such an evil one. Not many people, but some people, have the power to do such things.

Jack Fiddler, after defeating a windigo, put stakes in the ground and pulled its body through them. Another thing Jack did, after he strangled a windigo, was to make a hole in the ground and then set fire over the grave; to destroy the windigo.

I heard a story of Jack Fiddler going against a windigo. This story happened in the Setting Net Lake area.

The people in camp looked over a hill and they saw a red cloud – it was something powerful – coming toward them. When they saw this, Jack Fiddler was going out to meet this windigo. He had picked up a small axe hatchet; that's all he had to meet a windigo.

When Jack met that windigo, the people that were looking from the camp where Jack had started from heard strange voices shouting:

'Hit him on his neck!'

'Hit him on his neck!'

These people didn't know who told Jack to hit the windigo on the neck but it was a protecting spirit talking to him. Afterwards, the red glowing cloud disappeared because the windigo was defeated. Soon, Jack returned to the village. The only thing Jack told the people was: 'Don't go over there right away.'

* * *

Another story I heard about Jack Fiddler was told to me by Adam Fiddler, his son.

This man who lived in a tent was going to turn into a windigo. This man started to turn windigo; ice pressured, scraped, crunched inside this man's body. People heard this happening. This man was taking real deep breaths. He was getting ready to scream and in the moment that he would scream, he would be windigo.

They called Jack Fiddler and he came running right away. He picked up two cans and just banged them together and started singing outside this man's tent. When Jack entered the tent, he continued to sing while the man just stood there. Then Jack grabbed this man and threw him on the ground. The man got up and Jack threw him down again. The man was trying hard to scream but ice came out of his mouth and there was no sound. When ice came from the man's mouth, Jack dragged the man outside the tent and dropped him on the ground. Then Jack took a whip and he whipped the man. Jack told the man turning windigo:

Edward Rae, 1974. Photo, James Stevens.

'If you keep doing this thing, I'll whip you to death.'

As Jack was whipping this man, he talked to him and scolded him: 'If you turn into a windigo, I'm going to kill you. I have the power to do it!'

After this, this man who was called Wahtup, the Root, never turned into a windigo.

***

In fall, 1891, the wind was bone-cracking cold around the shores of Island Lake, Sandy Lake, and Windy Lake. At Island Lake, the lake suddenly iced over on November 7th and Big Bill Campbell's HBC men lost their nets under the freeze: winter early and hard set on Mother Earth. Activity at Campbell's HBC store slowed. All the clan families were out in their winter camps. Then there are some early winter visitors to the post from over the long portage. Campbell relates in his journal: 'Jack Fiddler's sons and Sinawackacappo came here last night, the report from the Band that an old woman is turned Canabil and has made attempts to commit suicide therefore the whole band is unable to hunt.' Campbell sent sixteen ounces of Scotch whisky to Jack Fiddler for a cure for the woman, who is one of the wives of the departed Porcupine. In the following summer, Jack Fiddler told Big Bill the medicine worked well. He had poured some of it into the fire as a burnt offering for assistance from beneficient other-than-humans in the forest.

On the forest winter trails of 1893, another event is reported at Island Lake that has a marked effect on Thomas Fiddler's family. In March, two Sucker clansmen, Sinawackacappo and William Mamakisickum return to Island Lake: 'They report Enos Loonfoot dead, having shot himself by accident while pushing sled with his gun.' Lament sounds from the drums of the Sucker clansmen for Enos Loonfoot was the eldest son of Loonfoot.

No one hunts furs when an immediate member of the clan dies. This custom of not hunting when there is a death is at least as old as the fur trade. But fur returns at Island Lake in the year of Enos Loonfoot's death in the Sandy Lake forests from other clans were good; consequently, in August, 1894, Big Bill Campbell decided to build an outpost on Narrows Lake. He ordered James Kirkness to build it.

James Kirkness, a half-breed, was the son of an HBC Scot and a Norway House clans woman. When James was born to her, he was, 'no-good,' a bastard in Christian view. He was unwanted by all but the old clansman, a powerful shaman, it is said. The old man taught him to see the ways of the forest. Then, later, James was adopted by the Reverend Enos Langford, a Methodist Missionary. Langford taught young James to read and write English and taught him the fundamentals of Christianity. In 1889, James Kirkness was hired as a servant and sent to Island Lake to work for Tom Linklater.

Big Bill Campbell had second thoughts about sending Kirkness off to Narrows Lake to take charge. This lake was five days beyond Island Lake by canoe. 'I put Kirkness in charge of this outpost though I did consider that he would be successful. He appears to be afraid of offending the Indians.'

The outpost that Kirkness built in the summer of 1894 with the help of Sucker, Pelican and Crane clansmen, consisted of a log house with two clay fireplaces, built back to back. There was also a half house, half wigwam for the hunters while visiting. Kirkness' post was built in a grassy clearing surrounded by large beautiful birch trees, off a small rocky point on the south side of Narrows Lake. (Narrows Lake is so called because it has several narrow channels in it.) This outpost was the first trading post in the upper Bay River lakes in over sixty years.

Now, Jack Fiddler and the Sucker clan; his allies, Adam Meekis and the Pelicans; the Crane clan and others had a winter outpost to resort to. The outpost in the birch clearing, was only open a few days a year when Kirkness was visiting. It was also very limited in its selection of supplies so Jack Fiddler and the Sucker clan still visited Island Lake every summer for goods.

It was 1894 that the younger brother of Jack Fiddler, Peter Flett made his last visit to the Island Lake post. At the west end of Caribou Lake Flett lost his self-control and began turning windigo. Flett's family had been travelling with the sons of the Pelican clan leader, James, Joseph and Lucas Meekis along with John Rae. When Flett began to manifest himself as windigo, he was destroyed and his body burned by these hunters. Peter Flett became the first son of Porcupine to die a poor death. At least, he was to die in the Bay River forests.

Hunting for furs beyond the long portage down into the Bay River basin at Sandy Lake, Narrows Lake, Cliff Dweller and Windy Lake appears to take an upswing in return from 1895-97. Some hunters, like James Meekis, of the Pelicans, caught majestic silver fox. Lynx were in number, suggesting that rabbit populations were strong too. 'Most of his Indians,' Robert Whiteway, the new HBC Chief at Island Lake, said of James Kirkness, 'are doing pretty good on the Fur there & paying up their Debts better.' In fact, trade went so well, some clansmen, 'paid their new debt and some of their old also.' The hunt for fur continued good returns through 1897. Sucker clansmen, Joseph Mooniyas, Sinawackacappo, and John Mamak-isickum, brought in 400 MB (Made Beaver) in Lynx. James and David Meekis of the Pelican clan from Caribou Lake brought in 'mostly lynx' as well.

The clans of Jack Fiddler and the Crane clan from Cliff Dweller Lake continued to live well. Plentiful fur gives meat and credit for trade supplies. In the winter of 1897-98, James Kirkness dog sleds out to Narrows Lake four times and Whiteway's journal reads: 'The Sandy Lakers had done very good on the Hunt. All the S. Lake Furs brought down this trip, two good sled loads.'

All seemed well to Robert Whiteway, who evaluated the forests and the clans strictly by his account books.

Just after break-up in 1898, a special visitor came to Whiteway's HBC post at Island Lake. He is J.K. McDonald, the Scot HBC Chief Factor from Norway House, who is travelling to all the posts inspecting his managers. When McDonald departs from Island Lake, he decides to go to Little Grand Rapids by travelling through the Bay River to this HBC post. He will be the first western person to travel this route in a century. Of course, he has only a faint notion about the long winding route to Little Grand from Narrows Lake. When he arrived at Kirkness' outpost he asks Jack Fiddler to guide him down to Little Grand.

The forest and water trail is some fifty portages long from Narrows Lake to Little Grand, depending on the depth of river flow. Jack Fiddler, who has now seen at least sixty-five winters, offers to take McDonald there. From this journey, McDonald tells us much of the man that is clan leader of the Sucker people.

It happened that on leaving Sandy Lake that the postmaster (James Kirkness) in charge sent us off without bacon, a very important oversight, for at least, we had a six day journey before us and possibly an eight or ten days' journey (to Little Grand Rapids).

I only knew of the want of the bacon when we had finished our first day's journey as the only food we had was flour, bacon and tea (at the Narrows Lake post). The absence of bacon was almost sufficient to cause us to go back to Sandy Lake for some. This would mean one day there and another day to get back, a loss of two days. So at my request Jack Fiddler and his two sons went on with me. We shot nothing on the way but we got a small quantity of pounded fish kindly given to us by an Indian family we met.

One day we lost the road or proper direction and at midday meal of cakes and tea I overheard Jack Fiddler's sons propose to him the advisability of returning to Sandy Lake. I not only overheard the discussion but I saw the man. Both sons argued him to turn back.

Their plea was good. It was, 'the flour is getting small; we have no bacon and we have lost the way.' Jack Fiddler dropped his head for a little then raised it and said, 'I cannot do that. I have promised to take him to Little Grand Rapids and I am going to do it, even if you two leave us. He and I will get there if we have to walk.'

Which meant that if his sons stole away with his canoe, still he would see me through on foot. The sons, however, seeing the determination of the father, continued on and we eventually got to our destination. On parting with me on the return journey to Sandy Lake and on bidding me good-bye, he wept.[7]

It was late fall of 98 when Jack Fiddler – after his trip to Little Grand – and the Sucker people came down to Island Lake for winter supplies. On September the 30th, they return for the Bay River forests, carrying '7 pieces Goods' for the Kirkness store. The birch and poplar trees have started to yellow. It was the beginning of another starving time – the worst days to be seen in three-quarters of a century by people at Island Lake, Sandy Lake, Windy and Caribou Lakes.

James Kirkness went out to his outpost on Narrows Lake early in October and when he returned on the 17th, he reports he had to 'brake ice both going and coming back!'

From this day, words of the suffering appear in the Island Lake Journals.

December 2, 1898, 'Kirkness got back this evening from Sandy Lake his Indians are doing very little on the hunt believe they are starving as there are very few Rabbits.'

January 10th, 1899, 'Sandy Woods camp they are still starving James & Alex Mason in last night brought about 40 MB Fur They are starving & not able to hunt & have supplied them some provisions.'[8]

On January 30th, Thomas Knott and Charles Hastings arrived 'all sick & starving.' When Kirkness' dog sleds in from Narrows Lake on February 7th, he says that the hunters are doing 'middling on the hunt.' When he returns from a March trip to Narrows Lake he reports 'didn't see any of the Cranes the others are doing very little on the hunt as they are starving.' The very next day, March 10th, Whiteway's journal reads:

'McKay & a Boy also in last night doing nothing on the Hunt they are starving gave them some provisions & to keep the life in them poor McKay is nothing but a skeleton.'[9]

On April 1st, Wallace Day and his son William, of Island Lake, arrive at the post starving. It is a hard, hard winter. A story of it is told by one of Thomas Fiddler's friends, William Mamakeesik.

* * *

William Mamakeesik: Adam Fiddler told me this story.

People were starving and Jimmy Kirkness said he would come to the shore at Narrows Lake, on a certain date. There was a misunderstanding over the date. The people waited and waited there and starved. It was very cold and so much snow; trees were bent down from the weight of the snow. Rabbits wouldn't come out. It was just so cold for everyone. Everyone was starving and everyone just lying on the ground at the old house there.

They didn't know whether there was any food in the store but someone broke in there. They didn't find anything except some pemmican. It wasn't very much. And there was a fat block from a moose.

They ate the hard bits off the pine trees, and usually only partridges eat those.

There was just one man living further up on Narrows Lake. The man who was living there was Loon Foot. Adam tried to go there to get some food. When Adam got there he was so disappointed, the family had moved out.

Adam was walking around on O'pasquiang Lake and he saw smoke. He walked over there and found the family had moved there. When he walked across the ice, he saw a fish net; he saw blood on the snow so he was sure there was fish there. He was certain he was going to get some food.

When he arrived, this old man, Loon Foot, fed part of the fish stomach to Adam. They had fish head soup and this is what they fed Adam.

This old man told Adam they had a lot of fish; his children were fishing too and they caught a lot of jackfish. They weren't hungry.

Loon Foot told Adam to invite all the people to come to his camp and fish.

When Jimmy came the people were almost starved. They didn't have anything. Jimmy said they should have broken into the store as soon as they got there.

After Jimmy came the people were feeling better. Then they moved over there to fish with that old man. He wanted them to come over there.

* * *

In the winter 1899, Island Lake reports that the Sucker and Crane clans are unable to find many fur bearing animals. The caribou will not come in numbers to Angekum. By late January we hear Jack Fiddler's people are living in scarcity.

At the end of the moon of mid-winter, Jack Fiddler's Sucker people and the Cranes know that James Kirkness will return to his outpost. There, they will get a few supplies for the few furs they have taken. Jack Fiddler and some Sucker hunters leave their camps around Windy Lake and snowshoe forty miles down the lakes and rivers to Narrows Lake. Sitting In The Sky, of the Cranes, and his men walk from their grounds and head to James' store also.

When the Sucker people arrive at the store, however, there is no sign of the Cranes. They should have arrived. It is thought that they too are starving and do not have the strength to walk to Narrows Lake. Camped among the birch trees at the HBC outpost, the Suckers await the arrival of Kirkness. Then it is reported that he is coming from the west, over the snow furrows of Narrows Lake, with two dog teams and five men in his party. Some strangers are with him: Reverend Frederick Stevens, a Methodist missionary, Peter Murdock of God's Lake and one hunter from John Wood's camp.

This will be Stevens' first meeting with Jack Fiddler and his Sucker people. When Stevens comes up into the clearing at the post, he sees how poor the hunters are. The younger Sucker men are wearing coats 'made of Hudson Bay blankets but all others were dressed in old, badly worn rabbit skin clothing.' They are all hungry from eating pine bark. 'Rabbits and fish were almost not to be had.' The Sucker clansmen immediately ask the Reverend Stevens for tobacco, to smoke to the other-than-humans. To this request, the white-haired missionary laughs and says in Cree: 'I thought you wanted me to bring religion and you want tobacco!' Later, after a perplexing service, Stevens asks the Sucker people to ask him questions about Christianity. At this, Jack Fiddler reaches annoyance. What questions could be asked? And he replies for the people: 'You just start at the first and tell me what you know.' Then, Jack Fiddler, clan leader, implies it probably won't take young Stevens very much time to tell him. Jack Fiddler, who traded into Big Trout over forty winters ago, is very skeptical of a missionary trying to press his strange beliefs upon the Sucker people.

Thomas Fiddler tells us what he thinks of the missionary that has come visiting at Narrows Lake.

* * *

Thomas Fiddler: Did you ever see the big Bible, the first part? I read of Genesis, about what Manitou did to create this world; what He did to make this earth and how he made light. That's what it says in the Bible.

The very first thing I said after reading this was: I believe that Manitou made the light. I also believe that Manitou made every human being, birds, plants, animals and the fish. I also believe he made the White men and the Indians.

Manitou gave ways of life to these humans, Indians and White men.

And I'm going to ask you one question.

The very first time a minister came to see the Indians and all the things that Manitou gave the Indians for their way of life – as soon as the minister saw how the Indians lived, he told them to throw it all away.

Now, when Manitou made this earth, the White men never saw the Indians for thousands of years. But Manitou made them both. I would say that Manitou did not make a mistake in doing this. I believe that before Manitou made this earth he thought about it very seriously; this is why I ask a question:

Did Manitou make a mistake by not giving the Indians the Bible?

I heard another story about a minister when he was over at Norway House, when he first tried to teach the people to pray.

At that time they were still performing ceremonies. The minister told Jack Fiddler, when you pray to God, ask him for anything that you want or need. 'That night' Jack said, 'I sort of prayed too. I asked Him to give me some big fat whitefish instead of all those lousy little fish I had been catching. That morning I went out and checked my net but all I had were those lousy little fish.'

'The next night I asked the Lord again for some big fat whitefish and I reminded Him that all that I had caught that morning was those lousy fish. And if I did not have whitefish tomorrow, I would perform shaking tent and get them that way!'

I guess you can see what I am trying to get at when the first missionaries tried to teach the people to pray. This was how the people reacted. They misunderstood in many ways.

* * *

In the freezing dusk, after this encounter between Jack Fiddler and the missionary, four of the Cranes stagger into the Narrows Lake outpost. They are Sitting In The Sky and Jacob Linklater, with two others. In intense cold, these men have travelled five days and four nights. During this time, they have eaten only one small jackfish. Once in the warm Indian house, their bodies tremble so badly they can hardly hold cups of tea. Few Cranes will be coming to the store. There is no food in their camp and people are too weakened to travel. [10]

The next day the Suckers and Crane people trade their furs with James for supplies but they don't receive much. Stevens feels the trading practises are Robert Whiteway's doing. It will cause Stevens to write in his Missionary Report from Oxford

House in 1899-1900 of the 'evil influence' of Robert White-way, HBC manager at Island Lake, who is Kirkness' boss.

The next morning Kirkness and the missionary leave the store and return to Island Lake. It is the moon of February, 1900, a cold moon that is often called the moon of hunger. And there is a famine in the Bay River country: a hunter and his son leave the Narrows Lake post to go out on their trap line for seven nights. They carry no food and no weapons. They take only a fish hook and snare twine to survive with.

The supplies people obtain from James Kirkness do not last long in the upper Bay River country – people were already starving when they got them. When this food is gone, people in Sitting In The Sky and Jack Fiddler's camps eat leather, bark, and lichen off the rock outcrops, but this food gives little strength. Everyone grows weak. Eventually, men sicken and cannot leave their lodges to hunt. When this happens in a family, all but the very strong are doomed.

* * *

Thomas Fiddler: It was a time when we had a coldest winter and no-one could hunt because the flu came around. Game was scarce. They had no nets for fishing, only hooks.

At the end of February, the people scattered and moved their camps. They – the families – spread out from Narrows Lake and drifted down toward Cliff Dweller Lake.

They couldn't fish in Sandy Lake.

There was one man and woman who had a child, a boy. They stayed near Narrows Lake when everyone left. Later this man, K'atchup, decided they would move south too. Their child, when he grew up, was called Joseph McKay. The woman was called Kichi Kakapetikwe. She was a sister of Peter Kakagamick. K'atchup had a brother named Adam Rae.

Finally, K'atchup left with his family during the bitter cold. They carried their supplies on their backs. About halfway to Cliff Dweller Lake, K'atchup collapsed. He had the flu and had nothing to eat. His wife made camp and built a fire to keep him warm. She didn't want to leave her husband. But, eventually, he died of starvation.

The other families didn't even know K'atchup had left Narrows Lake.

The wife stayed at the camp and rolled up her husband's body in a blanket. She couldn't bury him. She couldn't leave the camp because her child was too young.

She went down to the lake and chopped a hole through the ice, but it wasn't often that she caught fish. About the middle of March, the fish got scarce. She used the same hole all the time and the fish got scared away. The woman really had a hard time trying to survive.

She kept the boy wrapped up in her rabbit skin robe: she couldn't leave the baby by himself.

A man from Cliff Dweller Lake was heading for Sandy Lake and he passed through the place. He saw the woman there, barely alive and almost frozen. He took the woman and child back to Cliff Dweller Lake.

After the people went back to get K'atchup's body, they noticed the woman had eaten part of her husband's body. She smoked the meat before she ate it. James Campbell told me she ate part of the man's hips. The woman went mad and lost her head. She went about arguing with people.

After the woman recovered from starvation, she started to grow fat. The boy, Joseph McKay, grew fat too.

This woman lived to be very old before she died.

* * *

After Thomas' story, the skies return summer birds and James Kirkness goes out to the Narrows Lake post but few people see him. Weakened, they can't walk to the store. When James returns, Whiteway writes in the Island Lake journal that: 'James did not see half of his Indians and those that were in are doing very little or nothing on the Hunt.' Later, in early summer, Whiteway tells us that: 'This spring believe some of the Indians out there Starved to death ... Kakekapeetum among them.'

It is a tragic year for the clans. Within the Suckers, Jack Fiddler and his sons, Robert Fiddler, Adam Fiddler, George

Inside the Wabinogamick, 1947. From left, Thomas Harper, Thomas Fiddler, Cam Currie, Francis Meekis. Courtesy, Ontario Department of Lands and Forests.

This photograph shows the interior of the Wabinogamick, a religious longhouse. This spiritual ceremony which has not been carried out since 1959, is possibly the most ancient form of Algonquian, spiritual rite. Little is known of it.

It was, however, a thanksgiving ceremony to the spirits of the universe carried out by people who lived the lives of hunters. One of its features was the communal distribution of medicinal herbs for all its participants. This ceremony enacted each spring was one of four ceremonies carried out during the year.

Fiddler and Jack's brother, Joseph and his sons, Thomas and Thompson, and their families all manage to survive on rabbits, bark and lichen.

But the drums of sorrow ring long in the early summer cycle of 1900, lamenting all the deaths of the past winter. Somewhere between twenty and thirty-five members of the clans die in the Bay River uplands. It has never been clear, Thomas says, because some hunters and their families just disappear in the forest snows.

If Jack Fiddler knew what forces would come upon him in the future, he might have chosen to die this winter, in the land of his ancestors. But on June 27th, 1900, he arrives at Island Lake. He is still the leader of the Sucker people. He is healthy and with fur; 'Showery weather Kirkness arrived today old Jack Fiddler & Son came in Company with him S.L. done very good on the hunt.'

Although Jack Fiddler and his clan have survived, news of the deaths in the other clans is heard outside the forest. It is the first time a newspaper has ever published anything about the people of the upper Severn. The Manitoba Free Press carries these startling words: 'INDIANS STARVED TO DEATH: MEMBERS OF SAULTEAUX TRIBE IN NORTHERN KEEWATIN PERISHED LAST WINTER OWING TO FAILURE OF GAME.' Reverend Frederick Stevens, writing to the Free Press on September 10th, 1900, gives only a brief account of the starvations.

> During the late winter and early spring of this year, between twenty and thirty Indians of the Saulteaux tribe, residing at or near Sandy Lake and trading into Island Lake HBC post died of starvation. Rabbits and deer have failed these people and although they eat even the bark of trees and so forth, yet they are not always able to sustain life during the long winters.

A journalist follows up the report by interviewing James Smart, the Deputy Minister of the Interior. Smart is quoted as hesitant 'about placing any credence in the story.... The time that elapsed between the reported starvation and the first published account of it leads Mr. Smart to doubt the authenticity of the report.'

'You may state,' Smart tells the reporter, 'that we have arrangements throughout the whole of the Territories (with Hudson's Bay Co.) that would prevent any starvation or even destitution among the Indians.'

The Honourable David Laird, the Commissioner of Indian Affairs in Winnipeg, contacts the Hudson's Bay Company. They have not received any starvation reports from the post manager, Robert Whiteway, at Island Lake. The Indian agent at Berens River is asked if he has heard news of starvings from the interior. He has heard nothing, replying, 'that the place is so inaccessible that no news had come from there.' Laird asks John McDougall, Chairman of the Methodist Missionaries around Lake Winnipeg, if he had heard of starvations at Sandy Lake. McDougall replies that he has just visited Island Lake in late August and has heard nothing of the sort. A move begins to send the Methodist missionary Stevens from out of the forest for this contrived falsehood.

In late May, 1901, missionary Stevens, wife Frances and little son Willie, along with William Grieve and Peter Murdock start off for Sandy Lake to see the Sucker clan. When the missionary's party returns to Island Lake post after several days at Narrows Lake, they leave the very next morning for Norway House. Adam Fiddler, Jacob Linklater, and the Crane leader, Sitting In The Sky, along with Stevens and his family start out on the long journey to Norway House – a journey of three hundred miles. They will report to the Indian Agent, Reverend John Semmens, of death that stalked people in the winter of 1900.

At Norway House, Semmens listens to the story that Adam Fiddler and the others tell, then he sends this assessment to the Honourable David Laird, the Indian Commissioner, in Winnipeg, on the time marked, October 15, 1901:

In reference to the temporal condition of the Indian of the District of Keewatin....

It is a matter of serious question why these people should be in a condition of chronic want.... There is room enough to allow a township or two for each family. The resources of the country have never been interfered with by the outside influences. No railway has frightened away the game. The advances of commerce have never robbed them of a square foot of territory. So far as we know the population of these Pagan people is not on the increase. Yet we are told that the country cannot support these few souls....

It is true that the normal condition of the Indian of this portion of Keewatin is one of hardship and privation judged from our standpoint.... To a sympathetic nature would come the shock of a rude awakening.

It is claimed that these people are so reduced that they eat bark from the trees and lichen from the rocks. Doubtless they would in time of need fall back upon these resources but it is a matter of everyday experience that when no special want is felt the children scrape the trees and glean from the rocks as are our own children might eat hazelnuts or acorns.

I believe that special destitution did exist in the winter of 1899 and 1900, and that fourteen persons died by the Chief of Sandy Lake and a companion whom Mr. Stevens brought from the country so that he might tell his own story. When he was asked if that was usual or abnormal, he replied altogether unusual. In fact there was a sickness and the hunters lingered watching by the sick until scarcity was upon them. Then when they did not move ... within required limits and so want and weakness ended in death.

... at intervals of seven years old residents say the rabbits mysteriously disappear. Naturally foxes, lynx and other animals ... disappear also and there follows a time of scarcity. But they return in increasing numbers later and plenty follows famine.

Indians do not like the dense woods.... To obviate these difficulties they set fire to the forests and conflagration follows, resulting in the destruction of thousands of the very animals upon whose lives a hunter must depend for food and fur, for subsistence and income.* Small wonder if want and hardship should follow.

I can well believe that Mr. Stevens was actuated by philanthropic motives ... it is also deservable that he reached conclusions at first which broader observation has considerably modified, yet his strong nature finds it difficult to recede gracefully from a position once taken....

Speaking from an experience of nearly thirty years, I cannot see that any dire necessity has arisen nor that there is any impending calamity. Last winter was a better winter than usual.... At the same time I do not claim that the commercial relations of people might not be vastly improved.... These things, however, in our judgement are more the work of the Christian philanthropist than matters for State interference.[11]

On August 6th, 1901, Adam Fiddler of the Sucker clan and Sitting In The Sky and Jacob Linklater of the Cranes arrive back at Island Lake after telling the stories of starvation at Norway House. Several days later, Jack Fiddler and his other sons and related hunters arrive at the post at high noon for winter supplies. Another season is coming to transform the forest. The next day, under cloudy and calm skies, four Crane Hunters and Mooniyas paddle in. When all these hunters from the upper Bay River leave for their home ground, they transport thirteen bags of flour and eleven pieces of trade goods back to Kirkness' outpost.

At Island Lake in 1902, the winter is better for the hunters: 'The Sandy Lakers are doing very well on their hunt.' But at the end of the moon of midwinter there is more hardship. James Kirkness slugging it out on the trail, tells: 'Sandy Lakers doing middling on the hunt.' 'The Cranes,' Kirkness believes, 'has been sick and some deaths among them.'

In the summer of 1903, it is learned at Island Lake that a

*The statement is preposterous. In reading over 100 years of HBC post journals, HBC men write only once that they suspected a forest fire was started by hunters.

missionary, Mr. Lowes, wants to take some of the clan children out to a school at Norway House.

Robert Whiteway, the HBC trader at Island Lake, tells that: 'Wm. Mooniyas, William Mamakeesickum and two others arrived today from Sandy Lake they brought children to send in to school.' The next day, June 15, 1903, Lowes and five canoes of children and hunters start north up Island Lake heading for Norway House. It takes great trust for the clansmen to allow their children to go so far off.

The survival of the Sucker and Cranes, their distant brothers, continues to be uncertain. This winter of 1904, is little different than most of the deep snows since 1899. There are few creatures to help people survive. After Kirkness went out to the outpost on Narrows Lake to see the Suckers and Cranes, he returns; he tells blankly, the 'Sandy Lakers are not doing very much on the hunt – believe quite a number of them are sick and some deaths among them.' It makes one wonder what the coming days hold for Jack Fiddler and his people.

In 1905, Big Bill Campbell returned to HBC Island Lake to take charge from Robert Whiteway. Whiteway was transferred to a smaller charge at Little Grand Rapids. When Campbell arrived at Island Lake from Oxford House, he made an assessment of the Island Lake and Sandy Lake forests.

'The worst feature I found at Island Lake,' Big Bill wrote, 'was that the Indians had been encouraged to hunt furs out of season, which bought at a low price received the same valuation as prime skins. This system was not in the interests of the Hudson Bay Company and was tending towards the ruin of the fur country. I had no difficulty in changing this ... the Island Lake Indians eager in the conservation of the fur bearing animals.'[12]

The question in terms of Jack Fiddler's Sucker clan was: *Were there any creatures to conserve?* On December 2nd, 1905, Campbell reports that the 'Sandy Lakers in with three sleds and brought two bales furs, mostly rats and common furs.' Then two days before Christmas Kirkness returns from Sandy Lake with 'very few furs.' When Adam Fiddler, son of the Sucker clan leader, and William Mamakeesik come into Island Lake in February of 1906, they have only one bale of furs for all of the Sucker hunters.

Spring thaws early in 1906 at Island Lake. Geese are winging north by April 17. Five sunsets later flocks of ducks 'are seen flying around the open waters' and then for five days the air turns hot. Winter goes away to the invisible. On May 23, James Kirkness and Moses Gore paddle east for Narrows Lake to close the post for the summer.

It is the easy time in the season: the rush of sturgeon in the Bay River; the ever present suckers crowding up the small streams; new supplies of spring herbs are gathered; the red and blue berries of midsummer; roasts of pickerel fish. Filled stomachs. It is the warm season for Jack Fiddler's and Sitting In The Sky's clans.

By 1906, Jack Fiddler, this fiddle-playing Sucker clan leader, is old. But he is strong in his limbs and his mind. Jack Fiddler travels still with his sons, who are full in manhood and they do not lighten his burden. Jack is a leader who carries his own packs to Island Lake each spring. We view him enjoying his life as he laughs often among his people. In his time he has been bestowed with five women, eight sons, four daughters. His immediate family, including sons-in-law and grandchildren, numbers in the sixties.

Then there are the other family headmen who are all courteous allies to Jack. The Meekis family of clan Pelican – James Meekis, Alexander, David and Joseph are mated with some Sucker women. Raes, the Sturgeon clan, are related by marriages. Mamakeesick's are related to the Sucker camp. Loon Foot, is also a Sucker and related to Jack Fiddler.

All these headmen are sharing friends in days of need and in days of celebration. Among these headmen, it is Jack Fiddler who leads the thanksgiving for life in the Wabinogamick at Mud Lake. Jack Fiddler is the leader of all these families in the Bay River country. His curing powers are well known. His reputation at Island Lake is awesome; strangers often fear him. Jack Fiddler once worked on the yorkboats between Island Lake and York Factory so he is known beyond his own forests.

Now in ebb of his forest journey, Jack Fiddler is one of the last leaders in North America who has never signed treaty; never accepted missionaries; never accepted hand-outs; never been defeated. This Sucker clan leader still directs the affairs of his people in the upland forests.

Jack Fiddler is probably in his seventieth winter. He would never be accused of harming a white man. This fact was irrelevant to Jack's survival. It was not an attack on white men that would destroy Jack Fiddler.

Forces from the country outside the forest start to focus on Jack Fiddler and the Sucker people in summer 1906 when William Campbell, returning from Winnipeg, stops over at Norway House. There, he has what he thinks is an informal story session with Sergeant Daisy Smith of the Royal North West Mounted Police detachment. Later, Smith writes to his commanding officer in Regina on October 1st, advising him that:

> '... at Sandy Lake, about three days travel from Island Lake, there is a band of pagan Indians and it is generally believed that these people are in the habit of killing one another whenever one gets delirious through fever or other causes. They are very superstitious and kill through superstitious belief not through malice. But from information I have obtained, I cannot get but one case that there is proof of, and that, Mr. Campbell gave me, but it transpired seven years ago....'[13]

Outside of the forest, across the grassy plains, at the R.N.W.M.P. headquarters in Regina, Commissioner Aylesworth Bowen Perry writes a return letter three days after Christmas. 'Please instruct Sergt. Smith to have a patrol made to Sandy Lake, as recommended in his report, and fully investigate the rumour as to the alleged homicides amongst these Indians. I desire a complete report on the trip....'

In Island Lake and east in the Bay River forests, another brutal winter haunts the Sucker families. January is now filled with many bright, clear, freezing days and there is 'very deep snow' in the forest and on the lakes. A few days after New Year's 1907, William, David and Alex Mooniyas report their people are starving, so Campbell gives them some flour and a thousand whitefish that he has stashed at Pelican Rapids. Campbell writes in his journal on the 8th of January: 'Very cold ... Wolves are numerous and bothering traps.' On the 9th, the winds are howling, 'blowing snow into drifts'; Sucker people came to the post with a few furs. Hunger is among their families. Later, Elias Rae from Sandy Lake walks all the way to Island Lake for supplies. It is the coldest day of the year.

On the 16th day of March, 1907, Constable J.A.W. O'Neill, rides his dog team over the packed snows to the Island Lake post. The word of his presence spreads quickly among the Island Lake hunters: a soldier has arrived. O'Neill stays around Island Lake for almost a month, making a few patrols out to nearby winter camps. Then on April 15th, Constable Cashman, another soldier, arrives from Norway House, coming in with an HBC dog team.

In the frost sun-up of May 9th, James Kirkness takes the soldiers, O'Neill and Cashman, southeast on Island Lake toward the inlet of the Banksian River. Their dog teams ki-yi out as they set out for the upper reaches of the Bay River Narrows Lake. It is a territory that soldiers have never before penetrated. It is territory that has never seen a permanent western settler. Territory that has not been ceded to the Canadians. It is the ancestral territory of the Sucker clan and their allies, the Pelicans, the Sturgeons, and their ancient brothers, the Little Cranes, and the Caribou people. It is to the land and lakes of these people that Kirkness and the soldiers journey.

At sunrise on May 11th, Kirkness, the soldiers and their dog teams start over the long winter portage that separates the Bay River from the Thunderbird drainage basin. All day, and half of the next morning, Kirkness leads the soldiers ahead on a trail that is only the width of a sled. The soldiers keep stepping off the trail, to sink in snow up to their waists, then they struggle to regain the firm path. Sometimes the dogs lose the trail, 'which means at least a half hour's delay as sometimes it is necessary to unpack and take the dogs off harness to right them again.' Overhead, the spring sun burns; they sweat and their feet soak and blister.

Near high noon on May 13th, they arrive at Kirkness' HBC

outpost among the birch trees on the south side of Narrows Lake. The next day, some of the Crane Hunters of Sitting In The Sky arrive at the post to tell Constable O'Neill: 'Several of the tribe died during the past winter, including, their Chief, who, according to report, died last moon – which would be between the 28th of April and the 4th of May.' Sitting In The Sky, the old leader of the Cranes,* is gone from his people.

The spring of 1907 then turns as if the north wind has defeated the warming south wind. On May 18, at Island Lake, it is: 'Very cold & storming ... no sign of spring yet' and on the 20th 'still cold very little thaw.'

This same day at Narrows Lake Constable O'Neill describes:

'Two Indians arrived, Robert and Adam Fiddler, sons of the Chief of the Sucker tribe. They said that the Band would come in to hold a council meeting as soon as the rivers opened and they could reach here by canoe, as it was impossible to come in at present owing to the condition of the rivers and lakes.'

'Robert Fiddler, the elder of the two brothers, told me that the Indians had decided to elect him Chief as his father was too old to travel around.'

'I told him,' O'Neill says, 'that the election of Chief would be decided at the council meeting.'[14]

Robert and Adam Fiddler return this same day for Windy Lake; unaware of the intentions of the first soldiers in the forest. As far as the Sucker people know, the soldiers only want to hold a council meeting with them and the Cranes, on June 1st, at Kirkness' store.

The weather remains cold. The river channel south of Narrows Lake opens then re-freezes on May 24. People who come to the post have to wade through frozen slush. It remains cold for three more days – as if north wind is trying to protect Jack Fiddler – then it rains heavily for three more days.

*The Crane Family in 1907 had 18 men, 54 women, 44 children for a total of 116.

On June 1st, the day selected for the council meeting, Jack Fiddler's Sucker people do not arrive 'as travelling any distance now was almost impossible owing to some rivers not being open.' It rains continually four more days, blocking the sky in greyness, erasing the low horizons of the Bay River country. The the weather turns to snow. The ice, though pitted and rotten in many places, remains on Narrows Lake and Sandy Lake.

Six sunsets after the soldiers arrive, fourteen men of the Crane family come to Kirkness' store, where they sit down around the warm clay fireplace. The next day a council is held and the soldiers talk about the laws of Canada and ask about any deaths that had taken place. A hunter, Norman Rae – tells the mounties that windigo has been destroyed by Jack and Joseph Fiddler, the previous fall. Rae is an eye-witness to the event, and the police order that he stay at the store with them.

The next morning, Robert Fiddler and eight men somehow make it through to the Narrows Lake outpost and ask the soldiers if they can have a meeting.

'I refused to hold a council meeting.' O'Neill says, 'until the remainder of the band arrived.'

During the night, O'Neill and Constable Cashman decide that they will go south, up to Caribou Lake and once there, arrest Jack Fiddler.

For the next three days, Robert Fiddler leads the soldiers south, up the Bay River and they arrive safely at Windy Lake, where some of the Sucker clan are camped. But the lake is not clear of ice and the party of three canoes break away ice near the shorelines as they travel on.

'Never in the memory of an Indian,' Robert Fiddler says, 'has the lake been frozen over at this time of the year.' It was June 12th, 1907.

On June 13th, old Jack Fiddler and his men are busy building birchbark canoes on the shore by their camps at the east end of Caribou Lake. It is noon when Robert Fiddler and the soldiers arrive at this Sucker camp. There is joy among the people. Visitors are at hand; the honourable red coat soldiers of the white people. 'Men, women and children came to shake hand with us.' O'Neill says, 'A larger number never having

74

seen a white man before; one of the men said to James Kirkness: 'I am satisfied now that I have seen a white man.'

The Sucker clan welcome these soldiers with open arms for they have nothing in their hearts to fear. There are no thieves, no murderers, no violators among the people of Jack Fiddler's camp. But the soldiers – these westerners in forests they know nothing of – feel differently and when they learned that Joseph Fiddler was away from the camp hunting, they decided to await his return, and have the hospitality of the people.

Two days later, Joseph accompanied by two Sucker men, canoe into the camp. In the afternoon, O'Neill:

'Called Jack Fiddler and Joseph Fiddler into our tent and explained to them the crime they had committed, and that they must come with us to Norway House. Warned them not to speak to anyone about the murder, not even to us, until questioned at Norway House.'[15]

Somehow, the Mounties learned that Angus Rae, Jack Fiddler's son-in-law, has been a witness to the death of the windigo and he is also told not to talk to anyone; that he must go to Norway House as well as the others.

The reaction of the Sucker clan leader to this ridiculous charge brought out a strong response. Jack Fiddler asked;

'What has your Great Father to do with the Sucker people? This is the country of the Anishinapek who do as they please in their own hunting grounds. The soldiers wish to take me away and put us in their stone house but I have twenty young men who do not wish that I should go ... What is to stop them killing you....'[16]

Cashman argued that many white men would come in their place; 'the Great Father will never forget an insult offered to the men who wear his red coat.'

Jack Fiddler agreed to go. He agreed to save his small clan of people. He agreed to trust the 'Great Father' of the westerners. Late that afternoon, the soldiers and the Sucker men start back to Sandy Lake where the council meeting will be held. The parties arrived back at Big Sandy on June 18th after 'rough passage' over whitecaps blown on the waters by strong winds.

Indian Graves at Caribou Lake, 1910.
Photo, A. Vernon Thomas.

That morning, a council meeting is held by the soldiers with eighteen of the Sucker men* present.

In the first business of the meeting, 'Robert Fiddler, son of Jack Fiddler, is elected Chief unanimously.' Then the police, through James Kirkness, explain to the Sucker men why they are taking Jack, Joseph Fiddler, Angus Rae and Norman Rae to Norway House. Jack Fiddler has committed a crime in the eyes of these men who know him not.

'Some of the Indians were very much affected,' O'Neill wrote in report, 'particularly the present Chief, Robert Fiddler.'

The Sucker men are so shocked and disturbed that they cry openly when they learn Jack and Joseph would be taken from the forest to a western world. Robert Fiddler tells the soldiers: 'Do not be hard on my father, for he is an old man.'

'While your people are with us,' O'Neill replied, 'they will be shown every consideration.'

The next thing that O'Neill tells the Sucker men is just as unbelievable and irrational as their insistence in taking Jack and Joseph away. O'Neill tells them that Canadian law allows each man to have only one wife.

Robert Fiddler, who has three wives, then asked O'Neill: 'And what am I supposed to do with my other two wives?'

'Well.' O'Neill speaks, 'you will have to support them and their children too.'

This, of course, makes no sense to Robert Fiddler and the Sucker men; if they had to support women and the children, how would they not be their wives?

'You have seen with your own eyes,' Robert Fiddler replied, 'that there are almost twice as many women among our people as there are men. If a man is allowed only one wife, what are the other women to do for husbands? This is very harsh law.'

Then, some of the Sucker men tell the soldiers that they have been told by William Campbell that his HBC men will come out to Sandy Lake and shoot them if they trade with the opposition trader, H.C. Hyer. O'Neill asks the Sucker men who Campbell

*The Sucker Clan in 1907 consisted of 23 men, 36 women and 73 children; 132 people total.

77

has said this to, but the hunters say no more. None want to be taken away over this threat. Then, the men ask if they must slave in the yorkboats for the HBC and O'Neill tells them, 'they could please themselves,' as far as that was concerned. The Sucker men then ask about receiving a treaty.

'I promise that your claim for a treaty will receive attention,' O'Neill told them.

Then, in the afternoon, O'Neill and Cashman and Kirkness canoed off for Island Lake, then Norway House, with the four hunters of the Sucker and Crane people – taking them away as prisoners – taking them out of ancestral forests, where hunters have survived for hundreds and hundreds of winters without help from anyone but Manitou.

The day of arrival at Norway House, Inspector E.A. Pelletier, carries out a preliminary hearing into the death of the Windigo. Inspector Pelletier writes immediately his findings to Commissioner A. Bowen Perry at Regina, saying:

> I cannot possibly send these prisoners scot free; I have to commit them for trial.... These people are not civilized in the least, in fact many of their Tribe have never seen a white man.... I feel sure that like all the Natives about here, they are obedient and only too ready to obey the White man's Laws. As it is these people know none of our laws. They have never been taught any, as no white man ever went in that Country, that is for the last century or thereabouts.[17]

The proceedings go on in the afternoon at the R.N.W.M.P. detachment at Norway House. James Kirkness – the only familiar face – doing the interpreting for the soldier men. Angus Rae speaks truthfully of what he has witnessed before the Windigo died at the hands of Jack and Joseph Fiddler. Angus tells the hearing:

> I saw the woman, the sick woman in my wigwam; she had very little life left in her; she could not speak; she yelled with pain. I saw Jack Fiddler hold the woman down when she was out of mind.[18]

Near the end of the hearing old Jack Fiddler asks Inspector Pelletier, 'not to punish me too hard because I did not know I was doing wrong and that if I had known I would not have done the deed.' Joseph Fiddler tells Pelletier: 'I was told to do it, the mother of this sick woman, she wanted me to kill her and put her out of her misery – that's all about that – I know now that I made a big mistake that's all I want to say.'

Then, Pelletier reads out the warrants, the Sucker clan leader and his brother are both charged with murder and it is not long after that Canadians hear of this charge through newspaper headlines. The western interpretation is read from east and west in Canada.

There are some who see the great wrong that is being done to Jack and Joseph Fiddler of the Sucker clan. No one knows this more deeply than Robert Fiddler. When Robert visits the Island Lake post later that summer, he tells Big Bill Campbell, 'The old man did not do anything wrong in strangling the woman.' Some of the HBC men see the way the native clansmen are being maligned in the white man's newspaper. L.R. MacKay, who lived among native people wrote:

Of one thing I am certain, the Indians are not guilty of blood-lust in their relationships to members of their own tribe. I venture to affirm that the children of the woman so summarily disposed of have been, ere this, adopted by every mother heart in the band. My experience covering a period of twelve years had led me to infer that the majority of Indians are actuated by more genuine love for friends and relatives than white people are.[19]

J.K. McDonald, the former Chief Factor at Norway House, whom Jack Fiddler had guided to Little Grand Rapids in the summer of 1898, writes to the Manitoba Free Press, claiming that he had first met Jack Fiddler at York Factory as early as 1870, and he speaks in writing:

A moment's reflection will, I think, show anyone the position, the trying position, of those living in an Indian tent where an insane or delirious person is. There is a fire in the centre; kettles of boiling water hanging over it; young children and helpless infants lying around – this particularly is a night picture. In the tent there is no place to lie down for such a one. The Indian as a rule has to hunt for his daily food for himself and family and often for aged friends and weaklings. When an unfortunate member of the band is stricken as above, the hunter dare not leave to procure food.... Under such circumstances what is to be done? Under a surgeon's knife, if a patient dies that is the end of it, with these Indians, they have but one way of disposing of the matter. Again be it remembered for the good of the many, they are hundreds of miles away from doctors and asylums. Again what is to be done?[20]

At least, it seems the men from beyond the forests are told that not all killing is murder. It is very strange that westerners in settled areas build huge wooden scaffolds; with nooses of heavy rope; hang healthy men and women before an enraptured audience; and this is not considered murder because it represents their view.

On August 20th, Superintendent C.E. Saunders writes to the Assistant Commissioner in Regina because old Jack and Joseph, Norman and Angus, have now been prisoners ten weeks and a trial has not been arranged. Saunders also raises the issue of the families of the prisoners and witnesses. Who is going to look after their wives and children? Unless all are let go before September 15th, there is no way of returning them to Sandy Lake until January. Then Saunders says:

I understand it is the intention of the Department of Justice that Commissioner (Aylesworth Bowen Perry) try this case. I would strongly recommend that if possible the prosecution be dropped. The Indians be sent back to their homes. It appears the evidence will not warrant a conviction....[21]

Sergeant Daisy B. Smith begins to have similar feelings about the captivity of the Sucker men. Smith writes to the

Commanding Officer in Regina on September 7th, when the prisoners have been in captivity for almost twelve weeks:

> I consider the best treatment these men could get would be a change, as they are now living a life which is foreign to them in every respect.... Jack Fiddler is very old, and appears to be troubled with faintness. He falls down and his heart and pulse are very weak on such occasions.... He has laid for hours in these spells and it is with the greatest difficulty that we have aroused him.... I attribute this to confinement and uncertainty as he wishes to return to his family this month.[22]

While Jack and Joseph Fiddler await the outcome of their fate at Norway House, they have two regular visitors, Reverend Edward Papanakiss, a Norway House Cree and Reverend J.A. Lousely, both Methodist missionaries. Lousely wrote of Jack Fiddler in his imprisonment:

> He has not the slightest sign of enmity or hatred towards men nor God, no rebellion or unbelief, he is a quiet dignified man who has lived his life with a clear conscience, doing nothing because of which Kitche Manitou will bar his existence to the Happy Hunting Ground.[23]

So there are men, men from the forest, who see more of the truth of Jack Fiddler. These are men who, through humanity and justice, would return Jack and Joseph Fiddler to the upper Bay River. But these missionaries and the police Saunders and Smith, do not now have the power to free them. But, Jack Fiddler has the power: he will free himself form the agony of capture. He has decided that Manitou alone will be his judge, not some stranger from beyond his lands.

On September 30th, after one hundred and one days of captivity, Constable Arthur Wilkins got Jack and Joseph Fiddler and the two Raes up for breakfast. About seven o'clock in the morning he walked the four men down to the river bank below R.N.W.M.P. headquarters at Norway House. It was here the prisoners made a campfire for their meals each day.

Constable Wilkins stood up on a large rock about fifteen feet from the Sucker clansmen. Joseph lit a fire and one of the Raes helped him. The other Rae prisoner strolled down to the river with a pot to get some water. For over fifty yards, Jack Fiddler walked in front of the policeman's eyes. When he neared the bush, he took off his assumption belt from around his waist and kept on walking. It was ten minutes before Constable Wilkins realized that Jack Fiddler was gone and not coming back. Constable Wilkins said, later, that his attention was focused on the other three prisoners, not the old man.

Coming to control his senses, Wilkins alerted Constable Saunders that Jack Fiddler had disappeared. A search began, but no one could find the old clan leader of the Sucker people. It was half-past three that afternoon before Isiah Day, from Norway House, found Jack in the bush. They called Sergeant Daisy Smith to a place about one-half mile north of the police barrack. This is what Daisy Smith saw:

> He was lying on a rock with his sash tied in a large slip-knot 'round his neck. The noose was made of the sash he was wearing 'round his waist. The other end of the sash was attached to a tree and passed around another tree. He was dead. Suicide by strangulation, on account of the wrinkles 'round the throat.... There were three wrinkles. There was a little blood on the right ear; it was oozing from the right ear. He looked natural otherwise. His eyes and mouth were shut. He had no appearance of having struggled. The body was straight on its back with the hands down.[24]

The Mounties carried the body of Jack Fiddler back to the police barrack. A coffin was bought and twenty-five pounds of salt dumped on his body to preserve his corpse until an inquest.

'I let him walk away,' Wilkins said at the inquest, but who can really say that Constable Wilkins had control of his own mind.

There is to be no dropping of charges against Joseph Fiddler. There had been too much sensationalism in the newspapers in the city encampments of Canada. Whoever tried this case, whoever prosecuted this case, could be certain people will read their names. Evidence or no evidence, Commissioner Aylesworth Bowen Perry of the R.N.W.M.P. was coming to Norway House. He was coming to get a conviction.

On October 7th, 1907, Joseph Fiddler, son of Porcupine, went on trial for his life.

PART THREE

JOSEPH FIDDLER

PART THREE

JOSEPH FIDDLER

What does the Sucker Band, to which you belong, do to
anyone who is sick and cannot be cured?

AT NORWAY HOUSE, the trees transform into patched yellow,
rusted brown and rich golds. These, among green pines, turn
in another changing of the season. The north wind speaks,
winter coming above Lake Winnipeg.

On October 7, 1907, in the elapsing time of Joseph Fiddler,
the western system of justice begins. Joseph, hunter among the
Sucker family and uncle of Thomas Fiddler, stands in trial at
nine o'clock in the morning. Everyone concerned is inside the
council chamber at the HBC post. The judge is Commissioner
Aylesworth Bowen Perry of the Royal North West Mounted
Police who assumes his position under legislation called the
stipendiary magistrate's court. The white men allow Perry to
sit as a magistrate in a court where his men will give evidence.
The crown prosecutor is D.W. McKerchar, a well known Winnipeg lawyer and prominent Liberal. Observing on behalf of
the Indian Department is C. Cromptom Calverley. Constable
Daisy O'Neill is clerk for the court. James Kirkness, the outpost trader among the Sucker people, is interpreter. He will
not be called to give any evidence during the trial: he who
knows the prisoner better than any English speaker does not
testify in Joseph's behalf. Superintendent W.H. Routledge, the
acting sheriff of the Northwest Territories, is present. The
court, as described by a Manitoba Free Press reporter at the
trial has the 'pomp and circumstance of a military tribunal
combined with the powers of a civil court.'

A jury of six men from the neighbourhood of Norway
House will decide Joseph Fiddler's fate. Charles A. Wilkins is
the foreman of those who try to determine justice.

The trial of Joseph Fiddler starts with the testimony of Constable William J. Cashman, who is asked if any white people live among the Sucker band to instruct them in the law. No one, is his answer. Cashman then points out the closest white people live over at Island Lake, is a distance of one hundred and twenty miles, by the winter trail, and two hundred miles by the rivers in summer. The only white people in the district are at Island Lake; William Campbell, the trader, and Mr. McKersie, a Methodist school teacher.

The next witness is Minowapawin – called Norman Rae by the traders. He is married to Joseph Fiddler's daughter. His father-in-law, Norman Rae says, is called Pesequan, but his nick-name is Chawanee or Sandy. Rae tells the court that he lives at Goose Lake, a branch of Sandy Lake, and that he belongs to the Crane clan. The Indian name of the woman who was killed was Wahsakapeequay, and she is the daughter-in-law of Joseph Fiddler. She had mated his son, Thomas.

Norman Rae was present one evening, in the time when berries were ripe, at the Sucker encampment near James Kirkness' HBC outpost on Narrows Lake when Joseph and his son, Thomas, arrived with Wahsakapeequay. Joseph and Thomas lifted the woman out of the canoe and carried her on two poles up to the longhouse lodging. 'She was very sick then; she would not be quiet' and some of the women held her down on the ground to keep her under control. That night, Norman went off in the forests hunting and when he returned in the evening moon, Wahsakapeequay had been moved away from the longhouse and placed behind a clump of willows.

McKerchar, the Crown prosecutor, asks about the second night Wahsakapeequay was at the encampment.

McKerchar: Did you see her, where she had been taken to?
Norman Rae: I went over during the night and saw where she was taken to.
McKerchar: Was she still delirious?
Norman Rae: Yes.
McKerchar: Did she have to be held down when you saw her there?
Norman Rae: When I went there, nobody held her down, and

88

the prisoner, Joseph, had a string – with the other man, the ogema, Jack Fiddler. The string was in their hands and the woman was lying there.

McKerchar: Was anyone holding her down?

Norman Rae: No.

McKerchar: She was just lying on the ground?

Norman Rae: She was lying on the ground but they had spread the cotton on the ground and laid the woman on it.

McKerchar: She was in that position when you first saw her at that time?

Norman Rae: Yes.

McKerchar: What happened then?

Norman Rae: Of the cotton she was lying on, they pulled up the end of it, and put it around her neck, and they got the string in one knot or noose, and strangled her.

McKerchar: Who was it that took the cord and strangled her?

Norman Rae: The ogema and prisoner, Joseph.

McKerchar: What became of it after that?

Norman Rae: When we got there, Joseph told me that I had to take the body over to the Company's place and bury it there.

McKerchar: What did you do?

Norman Rae: I dug the grave and after I had done the digging, I put birchbark in the bottom. Then I got sticks and put them across the body and more birchbark on top of the body. I put earth on it.

McKerchar: Was this a law of the band that was being carried out?

Norman Rae: This is the law from what I heard.

McKerchar: From whom did you hear it?

Norman Rae: I don't know – everybody said it.

McKerchar: Is it a matter of general conversation among the tribes?

Norman Rae: Yes.

McKerchar: Do you know anything about the white man's law?

Norman Rae: No.

McKerchar: Have you ever been taught to distinguish between what is right and wrong?

Norman Rae: I have never been taught.

Reverend John Semmens (right), n.d.

McKerchar: Have you ever seen a white man before this time of coming out of Norway House?
Norman Rae: I have seen a white man come down sometimes to Island Lake.
McKerchar: Did any white man ever speak to you about right and wrong or did they have it translated to you?
Norman Rae: No. I never spoke to them at all.
McKerchar: Did you ever speak to them about anything else?
Norman Rae: No.[25]

The questioning of Norman Rae goes on the rest of the morning and, soon after lunch, it becomes clear that the windigo died by strangulation, carried out by Jack Fiddler and Joseph while John Rae (Edward Rae's father) and Norman Rae held her arms.

Shortly after lunch, Angus Rae, Manawapait, a young hunter in the Sucker family who lives at the Trout Lakes, takes the stand to give evidence in the court. McKerchar, speaking from behind a droopy mustache proceeds to question Angus through Kirkness, the interpreter. McKerchar proceeds, trying to ascertain when, in time, Wasakapeequay was killed.

McKerchar: When did you see her last?
Angus Rae: Last summer.
McKerchar: This summer just gone by or the earlier summer?
Angus Rae: The summer before this.
McKerchar: At what time during that summer was it that you saw her last?
Angus Rae: About the middle of the summer.
McKerchar: Do you know the division of time into months and years?
Angus Rae: No.
McKerchar: Was it during the warmest part of the summer or was it when it was getting cool?
Angus Rae: It was not the hottest part of summer; it was a little cool.
McKerchar: Was it after the hottest weather had gone by or before it came?
Angus Rae: After the hottest of the summer had gone.

McKerchar: To what tribe did she belong?
Angus Rae: Sucker Tribe.

Then McKerchar pauses and decides to ask Angus about the second night Wasakapeequay was delirious, the night the windigo dies in the camp of ogema, Jack Fiddler.

McKerchar: When you went out there, where was the woman?
Angus Rae: When we went over there, she was lying by the campfire. Joseph Fiddler the prisoner, was there.
McKerchar: Anyone else?
Angus Rae: Norman and John Rae.
McKerchar: Where any of them talking when you got there?
Angus Rae: They were talking. Joseph and Jack Fiddler had a string in their hands.
McKerchar: What did they say?
Angus Rae: They were saying that they were going to strangle her and put her out of her misery.
McKerchar: Who said that?
Angus Rae: Jack Fiddler said it.
McKerchar: Who was Jack Fiddler talking to when he said this?
Angus Rae: He was talking to his brother, the prisoner, and to John Rae.
McKerchar: Did the prisoner say anything?
Angus Rae: Joseph says, 'It's all right.'
McKerchar: Did Jack Fiddler, the ogema, say anything else beyond that they were going to strangle her to put her out of her misery?
Angus Rae: No, he did not say anything else.
McKerchar: Nothing else while you were there?
Angus Rae: No, I did not hear him.
McKerchar: Did Joseph, the prisoner, say anything except that it was alright to put her out of her misery?
Angus Rae: He said: 'It's all right.' That is all he said.

There is a long quiet space in the court room. McKerchar is thinking about how he will proceed with his questioning. The jurymen along the far wall fidget nervously and whisper to each other. Kirkness takes a drink of water. Then McKerchar begins again, trying to discover the relationship of young Angus Rae to the ogema, Jack Fiddler.

McKerchar: Did you object to their putting her to death?
Angus Rae: No.
McKerchar: Did you say anything?
Angus Rae: I did not say anything. They were all older than I was and I did not say anything.
McKerchar: Would you be punished if you objected to anything that the ogema suggested?
Angus Rae: I do not know. They might.
McKerchar: Is a member of the band bound to obey the ogema, bound to do what the ogema says?
Angus Rae: Yes.
McKerchar: Is a member of the band bound to do what the ogema says?
Angus Rae: Yes. If the ogema tells me to do a thing I must do it.
McKerchar: What would happen to you if you did not do what the ogema told you?
Angus Rae: Something would happen to me.
McKerchar: Of what nature, of what kind?
Angus Rae: I do not know what would happen. Something would happen anyway.
Commissioner Perry: Good or bad?
Angus Rae: Bad.
McKerchar: From what source?
Angus Rae: I do not know what would happen. Something would be wrong.
McKerchar: Would it be bad medicine?
Angus Rae: I will be punished in some way but I do not know how.
McKerchar: By whom?
Angus Rae: I do not know by whom but I will be punished, however, some way.
McKerchar: Did either John Rae or Norman Rae make any objection to the putting of this woman to death?
Angus Rae: No, nobody made objection.
McKerchar: Was the woman lying quiet on the ground by the campfire?

Angus Rae: She was not quiet. She was lying on her back and rolling her head about and moving her hands.

McKerchar: Did she say anything?

Angus Rae: No, nothing; but she moaned sometimes.

McKerchar: Did she hear the ogema say that she would have to be put to death?

Angus Rae: I heard the ogema say it.

McKerchar: Did she hear it?

Angus Rae: She must have heard it but I do not think that she understood.

McKerchar: Did she say anything when the ogema stated that she would have to be put to death?

Angus Rae: She did not. She was not able to.

McKerchar: Did she make any sign or motion to indicate that she heard it?

Angus Rae: She was rolling about when the ogema was talking like that.

McKerchar: What was done with her then – after the ogema made this statement?

The court becomes silent again as Angus Rae thinks back to the night scene of over two winters ago when Wasakapeequay was destroyed to protect the people. Then, Angus asks for a piece of cord. When it is handed to him, Angus ties it into a noose, then pulls the cord quickly, tightening the cord to a knot. Then Angus starts to talk to Kirkness again.

Angus Rae: Before they put this string on, they put cotton around her neck.

McKerchar: Which one did it?

Angus Rae: Jack Fiddler put the cotton around.

McKerchar: Who put the string around?

Angus Rae: Both of them, Joseph and Jack Fiddler.

McKerchar: Was the woman lying still while they were putting the cotton and cord around her neck?

Angus Rae: No, she was not lying quiet.

McKerchar: What was she doing?

Angus Rae: She was moving her head. She was swinging her hands.

McKerchar: Did she move her hands to prevent the cotton from being put on her neck?

Angus Rae: She did not try to do anything like that.

McKerchar: Did she attempt to do anything to prevent it, or did she say anything?

Angus Rae: No.

McKerchar: Did she make any noise?

Angus Rae: She made the same noise she did before.

McKerchar: Did the ogema give direction to the prisoner, Joseph, as to how the cotton and cord should be put on?

Angus Rae: The ogema gave directions. He said: 'We will put the cotton around so that the cord will not cut the flesh.'

McKerchar: Do you know why the woman was put to death?

Angus Rae: My wife told me that people were saying that the woman was going to turn into a cannibal. The people in the wigwam were saying this.

McKerchar: Was it before of after the death that your wife told you this?

Angus Rae: Two days after the death.

The mention of windigo causes McKerchar to stop questioning. He looks back over the transcripts and asks some things to be read back to him. When he begins, he does not ask about windigo. He decides to find out how much Angus Rae knows about white men.

McKerchar: Did you ever see any white men before you were brought in here by the officers of the Royal North West Mounted Police?

Angus Rae: I saw a missionary once, at Sandy Lake.

McKerchar: Who was the missionary?

Angus Rae: Mr. Lowes.

McKerchar: How long was the missionary there at that time?

Angus Rae: I do not know how long he was there, I saw him for half a day anyway.

McKerchar: Did the missionary talk to your band at that time?

Angus Rae: Yes.

McKerchar: Did you understand what he was saying?

Angus Rae: No, I did not understand.

William 'Big Bill' Campbell (1866-1948),
York Factory, 1910. Courtesy, Manitoba Archives.

McKerchar: Was it translated to the band?

Angus Rae: Yes.

McKerchar: What was the missionary discussing? What was he talking about?

Angus Rae: I do not know what the missionary was talking about. I was not well at the time.

McKerchar: Do you know anything about the white man's laws?

Angus Rae: No.

McKerchar: Did you ever hear anything said about the white man's laws?

Angus Rae: No. The only thing we ever heard about the white man was that he sent the Indians off to hunt furs.

The courtroom falls into silence after Angus Rae's assessment of white men. McKerchar shuffles through his papers, rethinking the evidence before he proceeds. All this time, Joseph Fiddler has sat on a straight backed chair beside a guard. His face is impassive and he shows no emotion in his face or eyes during the testimony of Angus Rae. Then, McKerchar looks up from his papers and begins to investigate the nature of windigo killings.

McKerchar: What does the Sucker Band, to which you belong, do to anyone who is sick and cannot be cured?

Angus Rae: One time I went over to the other camp visiting and I saw a man killed. One time, I saw a man killed named David. After they killed him they burned the body.

McKerchar: What tribe did this?

Angus Rae: The same tribe.

McKerchar: What members of the Sucker tribe committed the killing in that case?

Angus Rae: The prisoner, Joseph, was there and three other men: James Meekis, Joseph Meekis and Elias Rae, my brother.

McKerchar: Was the ogema there?

Angus Rae: He was not there.

McKerchar: Who was put to death at that time?

Angus Rae: David Meekis.

McKerchar: Was he a brother of these other two that you have named?

Angus Rae: He was their brother.

McKerchar: Did you see David alive before this killing was committed?

Angus Rae: Yes, I saw David alive. When I went to bed at night David Meekis was alive.

McKerchar: What more?

Angus Rae: While I was sleeping I heard somebody yelling and I went out and saw the body being put on the fire.

McKerchar: Did you see these parties commit the killing?

Angus Rae: No.

McKerchar: Was David dead before he was put into the fire?

Angus Rae: David was dead before he was put into the fire.

McKerchar: Why was David put to death by these people?

Angus Rae: I do not know why he was put to death. I was not there long enough.

McKerchar: Was he sick?

Angus Rae: Yes.

McKerchar: Was he sick at night when you went to bed?

Angus Rae: Yes, he was very sick.

McKerchar: How was he acting?

Angus Rae: He was sitting up and making a big noise while he was breathing.

McKerchar: Was he out of his mind?

Angus Rae: He, he was delirious.

McKerchar: Was he dangerous or was he likely to cause any harm to the people in the wigwam?

Angus Rae: No, I don't think so.

McKerchar: Was he moving or still?

Angus Rae: He was moving.

McKerchar: Was he speaking?

Angus Rae: Yes, he was speaking.

McKerchar: Could you understand what he was saying?

Angus Rae: He was talking but we could not understand him.

McKerchar: When was this?

Angus Rae: I could not tell, but it was four or five years ago.

McKerchar: Do you know of any other cases of sick people being put to death besides these two?

Angus Rae: I saw another man fixed the same way long ago.

McKerchar: How old were you when this took place?

Angus Rae: I was very small at that time.

McKerchar: In what tribe was it?

Angus Rae: In the Crane tribe.

McKerchar: Who was put to death at that time?

Angus Rae: I did not see anyone put to death, but the body was burned when I saw it. I knew of it because I was told it was killing.

McKerchar: What was the name of the murdered man?

Angus Rae: Askamekeseecowiniew. (Peter Flett).

McKerchar: Where was it that you say this body burned?

Angus Rae: Pretty near the other end of Caribou Lake and close to the Little Grand Rapids.

McKerchar: Had this man been sick before he had been put to death?

Angus Rae: This man was very sick when somebody brought him and landed him in one side of the wigwam where I was.

McKerchar: Who put him to death?

Angus Rae: I saw James Meekis, and his brother, Lucas, and Joseph Meekis and John Rae.

McKerchar: Were they the parties who put this man to death?

Angus Rae: Yes. They were the parties. I did not see who killed the man but I saw the body.

McKerchar: Did you ever hear the ogema give any reason for having people put to death who were sick?

Angus Rae: When they are sick and so long in misery they put them out of their misery.

McKerchar: Did you hear the ogema say that?

Angus Rae: Yes.

McKerchar: You heard him?

Angus Rae: Yes.

McKerchar: What ogema?

Angus Rae: Jack Fiddler.

McKerchar: Give the exact words.

Angus Rae: Jack Fiddler said that when anyone was sick like that and is so miserable they might as well put them to an end.

McKerchar: Did you ever hear them giving any other reason for putting them to an end?

Angus Rae: No, I never heard him give any other reason.

McKerchar: Did you ever hear the ogema say that anyone who died out of his mind turned into a cannibal?

Angus Rae: Yes, that is what the ogema says.

McKerchar: Did you hear anyone else say that?

Angus Rae: Yes, I have heard men talking the same way.

McKerchar: What men?

Angus Rae: All the men talk the same way, among them my brother, John Rae.

McKerchar: Did you ever hear the prisoner, Joseph, say that?

Angus Rae: Yes. I heard the prisoner say that more than once.

McKerchar: What would be the likely result if she turned into a cannibal?

Angus Rae: I don't know.

McKerchar: Would anything happen to the band if she became a cannibal?

Angus Rae: Yes.

McKerchar: What would likely happen?

Angus Rae: She would kill people.

McKerchar: Would anything else happen to the band?

Angus Rae: Nothing else but that!

McKerchar: To get back to the time of the murder in question, was the woman likely to cause any harm to the people in camp when you saw her first, by reason of her out of mind state?

Angus Rae: I cannot tell.

McKerchar: Was she strong or weak?

Angus Rae: She was pretty strong and two women were holding her down.

McKerchar: Was she strong or weak at the time you saw her at the campfire?

Angus Rae: She was pretty weak when she was at the campfire.

McKerchar: Were any others sick just about that time?

Angus Rae: Another man was sick at that time.

McKerchar: Out of his mind?

Angus Rae: Yes.

Commissioner Perry: What did they do to the out of mind man?

Angus Rae: This man was brought to the wigwam of the Sucker Tribe and the wife of this man was telling Jack Fiddler

100

to strangle the man. This was the wife of the sick man. The next morning I went out with my nets and my brother came down and I came up and he told me to come up quick. They were going to strangle a man; this man. And when I came I went up and I passed the wigwam where the sick man was. I went up right past the wigwam. I had a private job in the bush and my brother came to me. I came back to the wigwam; to where the wigwam was; the small wigwam. When I was going along with my brother, I saw a piece of string coming out from the wigwam and my brother told me to pull the string and I got the string and pulled it. And only then I knew that I had strangled a man.

It was Jack Fiddler who pulled on the line, the other side; the other end. After we had done I went back to my wigwam. I got frightened as I only knew then that I had done wrong. I had strangled a man. When I came back to the wigwam I saw the body wrapped up in a blanket. All the covering of the wigwam was pulled off and the body was lying exposed. I and my brother helped bury the man. We buried him four feet down. I did not make a coffin but I put in bark on top of the body. I laid cross pieces and put bark on that again and then I threw in the body. That is all.

McKerchar: After you pulled the string did you go in the wigwam?

Angus Rae: No.

McKerchar: Did you know who was pulling on the other end of the rope?

Angus Rae: Ogema, Jack Fiddler.

McKerchar: How did you know that?

Angus Rae: Joseph told me that it was the ogema at the other end. Joseph was in the wigwam.

McKerchar: How did you know the prisoner was in the wigwam?

Angus Rae: Joseph told me.

McKerchar: Which of your brothers told you to pull the string?

Angus Rae: John Rae.

McKerchar: Did he tell you what you were to pull the string for?

Frederick George Stevens (1869-1946), 1912.

Angus Rae: No, he did not tell me right then, but my brother told me down on the bank to come up and help strangle a man.
McKerchar: How long after the woman was strangled did this take place? How many days? Ten days?
Angus Rae: More than that.
McKerchar: Twenty days?
Angus Rae: About that.
McKerchar: The summer was getting toward the end?
Angus Rae: Yes.
McKerchar: Why, when you were asked before did you not tell us about this other man being killed this way?
Angus Rae: I was leaving this till last because they were Crane tribes.
McKerchar: Whom?
Angus Rae: That man.
McKerchar: What was the name of that man?
Angus Rae: It was Menewascum.
McKerchar: Had he any English or nickname?
Angus Rae: Yes, nickname.
McKerchar: What was his nickname?
Angus Rae: It was Piiwaapik.[26]

Angus Rae's testimony is a history of killing in at least fifteen years among the Sucker people. This is the end of Angus' testimony to a jury who sit in decision on whether Joseph Fiddler will drop from a scaffold at the end of a rope.

It is late in the afternoon but there is time for another witness, a man they say, who might offer an explanation to the supposed murder. He is Reverend Edward Paupanakiss, a Norway House Cree, who was in his youth, a hard drinking servant of the HBC.

McKerchar: What is your profession, Mr. Paupanakiss?
Paupanakiss: Indian missionary of the Methodist denomination.
McKerchar: You are a full-blooded Indian yourself?
Paupanakiss: Yes.
McKerchar: For how long have you been a missionary?
Paupanakiss: For 18 years since I was ordained. Before that I was a local preacher for 8 years.

McKerchar: Have you ever been in the Sandy Lake district?

Paupanakiss: Never, but I have been as far as Island Lake,

McKerchar: Did you ever meet the Sucker Tribe to whom the prisoner belongs?

Paupanakiss: Whenever I could, I met them at the post at Island Lake. I go there twice a year for seven years.

McKerchar: Have you ever met the prisoner there?

Paupanakiss: I never know him to meet him.

McKerchar: Did you ever meet the ogema, Jack Fiddler?

Paupanakiss: Yes, I met him.

McKerchar: Did you often meet him?

Paupanakiss: Three times I met him there.

McKerchar: Did you ever speak to the tribe when you were there?

Paupanakiss: Every chance I had. During the time they were there, they were calling for their summer outfit, we had service in the morning and evening. The longest they will stay there is 4 days and the shortest they will stay there is 2 days.

McKerchar: Did you meet them on each visit during these 7 years?

Paupanakiss: I could never meet them – only just when I went to Island Lake. I saw this tribe every summer for seven years, fourteen times altogether, and I used to hold service with them each time.

McKerchar: Did you speak to them in your native language?

Paupanakiss: A little. I used to ask them if they understood mine and they told me that they easily understood me. On each occasion I preached to them on religion. I told them it was not right to steal; that it was against the law; anything which the Book forbade, which the Bible forbade, was not right.

McKerchar: Did any of them ever express their beliefs?

Paupanakiss: The old ogema, Jack, with whom I had a long talk at Island Lake, stated that they believed their dreams.

McKerchar: What other beliefs did he express to you?

Paupanakiss: That that was their religion; their dreams are their religion.

McKerchar: Did he speak to you about delirious people turning into cannibals if they abide in their out of mind state?

Paupanakiss: I don't believe that he ever told me anything about it. I remember it from a very long time ago.

McKerchar: Have you any knowledge of their belief along that line gathered from members of the band?

Paupanakiss: No.

McKerchar: Where did you acquire that knowledge, from that band or from your general knowledge?

Paupanakiss: From when I was a boy I heard our own people; from our own people in our band; not from members of the Sucker Tribe.

McKerchar: What else took place at that conversation with Jack Fiddler excepting the long conversation on dreams?

Paupanakiss: That is all he said. That everything they dreamed was right for them; and that by virtue of their dreams and singing and conjuring in the tent that they would see meat, moose and deer. Jack Fiddler told me this. That is all that he told me.

Commissioner Perry: Did you tell them that it was wrong to take human life?

Paupanakiss: I do not remember that.

Commissioner Perry: Did you ever know of their tragedies which we have heard of this afternoon?

Paupanakiss: No.

Juryman Christian: Have you ever heard of them using poisonous medicines?

Paupanakiss: None that I have ever heard of.

Juryman Christian: I have heard it all over.

Paupanakiss: But when I go there, they never mention it.

McKerchar: When were you last at Island Lake?

Paupanakiss: In 1896.

Commissioner Perry: You have not been to Island Lake in eleven years?

Paupanakiss: No.[27]

Paupanakiss could probably have added much more to the trial evidence had he been asked the proper questions, but his long absence from Island Lake precludes any further questioning. So, at six o'clock, the court adjourns for an hour for supper. At seven, it will be Joseph Fiddler's turn to take the stand if he so desires. When the court resumes, Joseph is asked if he will give evidence. He declines and asks that Crompton

105

Calverley speak on his behalf. Calverley gives a short speech defending him on the grounds his actions were in accord with tribal custom.

Then McKerchar addresses the jury, asking for a conviction. He is followed by Commissioner Perry who speaks:

'As Mr. McKerchar has explained, murder is the intentional killing or taking of a human life. You have to consider the facts brought out. You have to find out whether the accused intended to kill the woman.... If you believe the facts of this evidence, Mrs. Thomas Fiddler came to her death through the hands of the accused. The law says that is murder. It evolves upon the accused to explain it to either by justification or in some way to reduce the crime to justifiable homicide or manslaughter.... To my mind the evidence is not clear on the customs of the Sucker Tribe.

'The missionary, the Reverend Edward Paupanakiss, was unable to give us any evidence other than what he had been told by chief Jack, but he said nothing about the treatment of the insane and the hopelessly sick. He discussed dreams and conjuring, but not all the beliefs of the Sucker Indian, not the actual belief of Joseph, the prisoner, and Jack....

'The only thing we have is the evidence of Angus Rae, in which he says that the accused told him that if the woman was not killed she would become cannibal and therefore a menace to the band.

'If you believe that you will have to accept it all. You will then believe this accused man was in the belief that if this delirious woman was not put out of her misery she would become a menace to the tribe by becoming a cannibal.

'Does pagan belief justify murder? You have to answer that. You cannot find anything but that Joseph Fiddler killed this woman.

'Was he justified in killing her because she might have turned into a cannibal? This might possibly be urged as a defense. The tribe was ignorant of the law of the land.

'We questioned both witnesses as to that and the impression left on my mind is that they do know what the law forbids....

'As to the question of pagan belief, if you find that the accused is justified in killing because of his pagan belief where will it land us if we accept such a belief? What the law forbids no pagan belief can justify. The law says: "Thou shalt not kill." He cannot justify his act by pleading it.

'However, you have a perfect right in spite of what I say, if you think that pagan belief would justify him, to say so, but consider first what the result would be. For as to his ignorance of the law that is a matter for executive clemency.

'Before committing his case to you, I wish to say that you can give anyone of these three verdicts: Guilty, Not Guilty, or Guilty of Manslaughter.

'I will now ask you to retire and to consider the verdict which you shall give.'[28]

The six-man jury retires and after some study they return to the court and ask for two definitions: guilt of manslaughter, and death from the result of self-defense. The jury appears confused. Perry defines self-defense as a killing that results from immediate danger and manslaughter as intent and loss of self-control. Juryman Wright then asks Perry if they are restricted to only three verdicts. Perry states this is the case but they can add a recommendation to any of these three verdicts. Wright then proceeds with another question:

Juryman Wright: Why did they object to taking the woman into the wigwam where the rest of the family was?
The Commissioner: There is no evidence to that effect.
Juryman Wright: Was it ascertained the distance the woman was brought?
The Commissioner: It was not ascertained.
Foreman Wilkins: Could we ask that question now of the witness?
The Commissioner: No.

Foreman Wilkins: Then the jury cannot come to any decision!
The Commissioner: Kindly retire again, gentlemen, and consider your verdict.

When the jury returns, the foreman, Wilkins, give the verdict: guilty of murder but with a recommendation for mercy, 'on account of the prisoner's ignorance and superstition.'

Joseph, who sits attentively through the trial, is asked if he has anything to say to the court who has passed the law upon him. Joseph stands up to speak to the court through James Kirkness, the translator.

'I did not know better. I am angry. I was in hopes I would be let off without being punished. I do not want my life to be taken away until my death comes. I wish that God had blest me. I have no wish to say any more.'[29]

Commissioner Perry then passes the sentence of the westerners on Joseph, hunter of the Sucker people.

'... The law does not permit me to exhibit any mercy toward you. It is that he who commits murder shall be hanged.... I can hold out to you no hope that a pardon will be extended to you. You have been found guilty ... by a jury of six men who have given you a fair and impartial hearing.

'The evidence which has been given before the court disclosed that this is not the only case in which human beings have been done to death by yourself and other members of the Sucker Band.

'The law says that this must be. The object of punishing you is not to prevent a death so much as it is to be a warning to the other members of your tribe that human life is sacred and cannot be taken.

'The sentence of the Court is upon you, the said Joseph Fiddler, an Indian, and known among the Indians as Pesequan, that you be taken to the place from whence you came, namely, the Royal North West Mounted Police Guard Room at Norway House in the Northwest Territories and that you be taken from between the hour of six o'clock in the forenoon and twelve of the clock of that day, to the place of execution, there, and that you be hanged by the neck until you are dead: and may God Almighty have mercy on your soul.'[30]

Two weeks later, Commissioner Perry, having obtained the desired conviction, completely reverses his opinion on what have been the customs of the Sucker people. He is writing to the Minister of Justice in Ottawa on October 30, concurring with the jury's recommendation for mercy.

> The accused knew it was wrong to take life under ordinary circumstances. He believed, however, that insane persons were dangerous to the well being of his tribe and that unless they were strangled they would turn into cannibals.... It is clear that it has been the custom of the tribe from time immemorial to put to death members of their band, and other bands, who were thought by them to be insane or incurable.[31]

In the following weeks, an Order in Council, based on Perry's recommendation, commutes Joseph Fiddler's sentence to life imprisonment and the Department of Justice drops any proceedings against Angus Rae, John Rae and the Meekis brothers.

In January, 1908, Joseph, now ill, is transferred to Stony Mountain where he is placed in the infirmary to somehow recover his health. Norman Rae returned to Island Lake and died shortly thereafter. James Kirkness left the Sandy Lake country, never to return. The HBC posts him to Poplar River on Lake Winnipeg. William, 'Big Bill' Campbell is transferred to York Factory by the HBC at the conclusion of the trial.

* * *

Indians survived without the help of any white man

AFTER CLAN LEADER Jack Fiddler and his brother, Joseph, were taken from their ancestral grounds by the R.N.W.M.P. in June, 1907, Robert Fiddler and James Meekis remain to lead the people through still trying times. The arrests of Jack and

Joseph were not widely discussed in the years that followed. Forest clansmen preferred to forget this humiliation. After all, nothing could be done against the forces of westernization that were sweeping North America, and the less than bountiful forests made it difficult for clansmen to concentrate on anything but survival. The best that could be hoped for was that Joseph Fiddler would be returned to the clan and his family of two women, two daughters and two sons.

At Island Lake, February, 1908, the news was disturbing for the clans. Two red coat soldiers, R.N.W.M.P., have returned again, bringing back young Angus Rae. They will dog sled east on Island Lake, up the Sagawitchewan River and over the long portage down into the Bay River. Angus Rae is to be returned and the soldiers, Inspector E.A. Pelletier and Constable Cashman, want to talk to clan leader Robert Fiddler. He will endure insult from them. In the minds of these western men, Robert is an ignorant man.

The soldiers come with HBC servant, Donald Flett, for their interpreter. Angus, away from his people for eight months, guides the party to the HBC outpost on Narrows Lake.

At the outpost, set among the snowed in birches above the shore of Narrows Lake, Paul Fiddler, manages the trade goods. He is the first of the Sucker clansmen to learn commerce. At the post, his brother, Robert Fiddler, meets with Inspector Pelletier. Robert, 'strikingly handsome' and powerful looking, is a man of about forty-four winters. For many years, Robert, along with his brother Adam, have been, in effect, leaders. But it is Robert Fiddler, the oldest brother that is hereditary clan leader. He will talk to Pelletier. Before this, Robert has spoken only to five white men.

Pelletier now speaks about this meeting. In his mind he sees the Suckers 'as the worst band in the district. They are murderers, liars and very crooked.'

He speaks his attitude in an insulting manner to one of the forest's most prestigious hunters: Robert Fiddler, son of Jack Fiddler, grandson of Porcupine Standing Sideways, a descendant of Yellow Sky, Long Fellow, Tinpot and Little Crane. He is clan leader in the forests that are unceded to the whites and their soldiers.

I spoke to them about two hours explaining the law.... I told the chief that if he did not change his ways I would put another chief in his place ... that we were friends of the good Indians and that bad Indians need fear us as we were numerous....

'They were not to think that because they were living in an isolated place we would not hear of their doings....

'I said that I hoped that the next time I shook hands with him I would be able to say, "I shake hands with a good chief." Pelletier also warns the Suckers that Angus is now a friend of theirs and that if they molest him in any way they will feel very sorry for it.'[32]

After the soldiers leave, Thomas Fiddler tells how happy Angus Rae is to be returned to his people. 'Angus went around shaking hands with everybody. It was winter, so Angus thought it was time to say "Merry Christmas" to everybody. He said "ahniken-Kismas" to all.' Angus tried hard to speak English now. He told the people the way to say *today* is, 'o'tay.' Of course, Angus can't speak English but he heard a lot of people speaking English. When he heard the word, yesterday, he pronounces it 'Keeask o-tay.' But in Indian, o'tay means, heart, and keeask o-tay means, seagull's heart.

Thomas also tells about the effects of the imprisonment on Angus Rae. 'He built a cellar under his lodging so that he can escape should the police ever come to take him away again. There will be a cellar in his lodgings for many winters to come. He will always fear the white man.'

Outside of the isolated forests of the Sucker clan there is much discussion about the imprisoned Joseph Fiddler. Many of the northern fur traders are shocked by the outcome of the trial. Although no one says so, all the traders know the trial was farcical. Six months after Joseph is locked in Stony Mountain, many of the notable men from Norway House sign a letter that petitions for his complete pardon. These men are: William 'Big Bill' Campbell – who reported the windigo killings; James Begg; James Garson and Henry T. Wright, who were three jurors in the trial; Crompton Calverly, Indian Agent at the trial; J.A. Lousely; Edward Paupanakiss; Thomas

Outside Courtroom, Norway House, 1907.
Constable Cashman, R.N.W.M.P. Norman Rae, Angus Rae,
Joseph Fiddler. Courtesy, P.A.C. Ottawa.

Ferrier and Alex Cunningham, all Methodist missionaries; Donald A. McIvor, a private trader with 31 years experience among the Indians; and Donald C. McTavish, A.A. Sinclair, E.J. Bivington, J.K. MacDonald, Donald Flett, John Taylor, all of the HBC.

In part, their petition for Joseph Fiddler reads:

> We have learned that the old man had been in the hospital nearly all the time since he reached Stony Mountain. He suffered from a very severe attack of pneumonia during the process of which no hope was entertained of his recovery. While he has partially recovered he is still in such a condition of health that he has almost no chance of living through another winter.
>
> We are not sure that you have had the opportunity of knowing that the entire band is in perfect sympathy with those, who because of possessing a little more nerve than the rest, are detailed to do the gruesome task. Their actions in this respect is the very opposite of what we call murder being undertaken sometimes at the earnest solicitations of one who has been delirious and regained consciousness for a time, when they would beg, even implore relatives to kill them, if they should relapse rather than leave them to run and risk of turning a wretched creature and a terror to men, never allowed to enter the Happy Hunting Ground. That condition is the hell of those Indians.
>
> Sir, we earnestly beg that you will do all in your power to secure his pardon.[33]

From the Department of Justice in Ottawa, a copy of the petition was sent to Commissioner A. Bowen Perry in Regina for his recommendation. Perry's short and hard reply is: 'While I agree largely with it, I am of the opinion that the prisoner should not be released too soon....'

Possibly Perry did not read, or care what one of the paragraphs said.

It was two years plus a day since Joseph Fiddler was arrested at Caribou Lake, when, in June, 1909, John Semmens of the

Inside Courtroom, Norway House, 1907. James Kirkness is at left, back to camera; Joseph Fiddler is seated beside the R.N.W.M.P. officer; D.W. McKerchar is standing at centre; Commissioner Aylesworth B. Perry is seated at back, left. Six man jury is seated far right. Courtesy, P.A.C. Ottawa.

Indian Department wrote to Colonel Irving, the Commanding Officer at Stony Mountain and offers to take Joseph Fiddler back to Island Lake in mid-July on the understanding that he will be released. To this request, A. Power, the Acting Deputy Minister of Justice in Ottawa, writes, 'I beg to inform you that it is not the intention of the Department to release this man at present....' Then, on July 26th, 1909, Joseph Fiddler, pleading for his life, dictates a letter through an unknown translator to the Minister of Justice.

To the Minister of Justice

Dear Sir – I desire to lay my case before you and ask that a pardon be granted me. I am fifty three years old and if I am confined here longer I will die, but I think if I can get back to where I belong I will live.

I desire to ask you not to look upon me as a common murderer. I was the Chief of my tribe, we had much sickness, and the sick ones were getting bad spirits and their friends were afraid of them and sent for me to strangle them. This was *not* common killing, for we never strangle a well person, neither would we dare to shoot, or stab a sick person. It has always been the rule of our people to strangle sick ones who went mad.

No one but the Chief of the tribe or one named by him could strangle anyone.

If you let me go back to my place I will teach my family and people the white man's law. I am sick now and can't walk, but I think I will live if you let me go home.

I will tell them how the white man lives. I wish you to consider that I am a poor Indian and don't know anything. I beg of you to remember your promise of last fall and send me back to my people before I die, and I will tell my people that the white man's Government always speaks true.[34]

In the late summer winds a third letter of petition for Joseph Fiddler's pardon is sent to the Minister of Justice, by Archdeacon Robert Phair of Winnipeg. Phair points out that he has been a missionary among the Indians since 1865. He was, in fact, the Superintendent of Indian Missions in Ruperts Land for the Anglican Church of Canada; and asks:

> ... if action can be taken soon, he might get out to the end of Lake Winnipeg before he is too weak and the season too far advanced.
>
> Hoping this message for the old man will be acceptable and result in his getting his liberty.

To Phair's request, comes an answer and freedom for Joseph Fiddler.

C.P. Telegram
September 4th, 1909

The Warden of the Manitoba Penitentiary
Stony Mountain, Manitoba

Governor General authorizes immediate release of Joseph Fiddler, alias Pesequan. Release accordingly. Letter confirming this message follows.

Thomas Mulvey
Under-Secretary of State Canada

To Under Secretary of State
September 5th, 1909

> In reply I beg to state this convict died of consumption on September 1st at 8:15 a.m. after being in the penitentiary hospital for 18 months.

A. Irving Warden[35]

Joseph Fiddler was gone to the spiritual world of the Sucker clansmen. Pardoned and released from prison by an Ottawa word paper. He had already been free for three days. The records concerning Joseph Fiddler's pardon contain no correspondence from Commissioner Perry authorizing approval. Presumably, he had not been consulted about the pardon. It is ironic that in 1909, the year that Joseph Fiddler died in Stony Mountain, Aylesworth Bowen Perry was made a Companion of the Order of St. Michael and St. George. For Perry, this British award for chivalry was a step toward knighthood.

As we sit and talk sadly about these days, Thomas tells about Joseph's family: of how they struggle to survive in the woods.

* * *

Thomas Fiddler: Joseph Fiddler, the man the Sucker people called Pesequan, had two wives. One of his wives was Charlotte Mamakeesik. I don't know the name of his other wife but they had five children. Charlotte had two sons, Thompson Quill, and Tommy Fiddler. The other woman had three children, two daughters, both called Mary, and another daughter named Jessie.

In this time, after the missionary came, the Sucker people were just taking English names. This was confusing and this is why Thompson Quill ended up with this name, not Fiddler. This is also why two of Joseph Fiddler's daughters were named Mary. They thought all white women were called Mary.

Now, when the white men took Jack and Joseph away in 1907 there was no treaty here, but there was a store. After Jimmy Kirkness left in 1907, two half-breeds looked after the store. When these guys left, Paul Fiddler looked after it but this store was very poor in equipment so often people went to Little Grand Rapids to trade. When the store on Narrows Lake closed, Paul Fiddler moved over to Island Lake. He never came back.

And when Joseph Fiddler never returned, Charlotte and the other woman had to raise their children alone.

It is true that Charlotte Mamakeesik was a very strong woman.

With only twine for nets and snares, and equipment, axes, hooks and ice chisels, they spent the winters roaming the lakes trying to survive. So these two women and Joseph's children caught fish from the open rivers at the outlet from Name Lake and at the inlet of the two other lakes. They built weirs in the rivers and caught fish there because the lakes were frozen solid. It was impossible to catch fish in lakes. They also caught fish along the river from Loud Beaver Lake.

In the summertime, they got twine from the store to make gill nets for fishing, and they camped on the shores of Caribou Lake. At the east and of Caribou Lake, they caught a lot of whitefish; it was their only way of surviving. At this place there is a small lake and a river running between it and another lake. It is called Owajosewayahink Lake. They fished at another lake right across Caribou Lake called Antamake Lake. This lake is filled with dark water so the whitefish in this lake are much darker in colour.

In the summer, Charlotte and her children would set up a wigwam. They would make a structure like a small wabino-gamick. They used moss and spruce to cover the frame. At night, they built a fire inside that made smoke to drive out the mosquitoes. When the mosquitoes all left, they would close the door and put out the fire.

Now it happened that when they fished too long in one place, they wouldn't catch fish anymore. So they moved across a portage to another river where they caught whitefish.

Joseph's family just kept moving about these lakes and rivers. These women, Charlotte and Joseph's other wife and children were about the only ones who lived this way. It was the only way they could survive and raise their children.

PART FOUR

ROBERT FIDDLER

ROBERT FIDDLER

The man who hanging was too good for

THE DEATHS OF JACK AND JOSEPH FIDDLER were an ominous prelude for a signing of treaty by the Sucker, Pelican and Crane clans in the forest uplands of the Bay River. These clansmen had long heard about the treaties western peoples in Canada were making with natives in different regions of the country. Survival pacts might be a better description of these treaties now that the ecological systems in the boreal forests were greatly diminished. The loss of beaver was especially important as a factor in the clans' survival. People had starved in the boreal forest all through the 19th century because beaver as a staple for winter food supply was now a limited source of protein. 'Hunger had a long arm,' and Robert Fiddler and his ally, James Meekis, had heard of the 1905 treaties signed at Osnaburgh House and assumed there was some value in signing one for their hard pressed people.

Now word was spoken that the clans at Island Lake would be taken into treaty in the summer of 1909. If there was doubt that this would actually occur, there was good reason. Treaty talk had taken place at Island Lake before 1891. Magnus Harper, an Island Lake leader, sent a letter to Angus MacKay, the Indian Agent for the Lake Winnipeg District, asking for treaty, as 'it would help us get a living.' Hunger and the vacant forests spoke for a treaty. In July, 1891, clan leader, John Wood, sent another letter to Angus MacKay at Berens River, 'We are very poor.... We have got no tools.... We want the Queen to help us.'[36] When there is no reply to this letter, John Wood again writes to MacKay in August, 1891. Winter is coming. 'We are very poor, very poor indeed, and our country too.... I wish you would come and make treaty with us. I wish you will try and help us.'[37] Eighteen years later, it appears that treaty will occur at Island Lake – now that it is in the interests of the powerful westerners to have a document signed.

The question raised for Robert Fiddler was: should the Sucker, Pelican and Crane clans sign this treaty at Island Lake if it should be presented? A treaty with the white men was only part of the perplexing difficulty faced by Robert Fiddler. What was one to think of the cruelty of these people who had so arrogantly taken his father and uncle off to their deaths? Their strange religion was another matter. Acceptance of it and its barbaric customs seemed necessary. Robert struggled hard within his mind on how he might protect the Sucker clan people against the outside world.

In 1909, Robert Fiddler journeys to Island Lake. Robert finds himself a marked man, with the HBC, and with the missionary. It must be difficult for a man of Robert's courteousness to accept the hard words that are used upon him by A.H. Cunningham, the Methodist Missionary who lives at Island Lake. Cunningham, the missionary, speaks:

> ... my experience with the Chief of the Sucker Band of Sandy Lake or the Fiddler tribe as better known on account of their blood thirsty cold blood murders of a couple of years ago, they have been the terror of the other Bands of Indians and also the HBC's post manager was simply at their mercy last year. When they changed the manager, a man who came down with us to take charge, an able bodied fear nothing and he certainly had it in for the Chief and did not have a good word to say for him but pointed him out to me as the man who hanging was too good for.
>
> However, it was well I new the worst on the beginning and at Island Lake he was up visiting and heard that a missionary was on his way down so he wanted to see me arrive so I entered into conversation at once fearlessly and plainly spoke hard at once against sin and crime as the great enemies of God and all that is good but always ended by telling that was simply the Devil in man and the Lord Jesus Christ who I came all this way to tell them

about was the remedy for all this and without him you can do nothing good.

After his attending half a dozen meetings and every prayer meeting he finally invited me to S. Lake. If I could fix a time he would come halfway and meet me.

I made a promise to have to go & he was to meet me or rather he me met half way. True to his word when we came to that most only Dense woods & mountainous 7 mile portage, his men & canoe was there waiting, having been instructed to take a net and simply catch fish and live there until I arrived. He was sure I would come, such is an Indian's confidence in the white man when once you have got him.

At Sandy Lake, Cunningham baptized sixty children and married some of the younger couples. He held a meeting at night under torchlights. With a translator he preached a sermon and 'Chief Robert showed great distress and true signs of a breaking up.' At another prayer meeting the next morning, 'Robert looked stronger and rather defiant.' Cunningham, this Sunday morning assaulted Robert Fiddler and the clan folk with the use of Timothy 1-15. The powerful and insulting suggestion used on Robert Fiddler was that law existed for the ungodly ... for murderers of mothers ... for manslayers ... for liars ... for whoremongers ... for sinners but 'Christ Jesus came into the world to save sinners.' The effect of these verses was: 'Robert amongst others were greatly shaken up, came near a crash but got away.' In an afternoon meeting Reverend Cunningham spoke to the clan folk from John 14. Finally, Robert Fiddler broke under this onslaught against boreal belief:

'O the mighty power of God, how it fell on Robert resisting till the water like great drops of rainfall, trying to hold up in the midst of his warriors but it was no use, he had to go this time, he sobbed, he tried to pray, he shook and what a sight I shall never forget I was worked myself pretty well ... his warriors followed from there, everything went from there in a flood time, they flocked in and around until I could not get away at night.'[38]

Reverend Edward Paupanakiss.
Courtesy, United Church Archives, Winnipeg.

Such is the experience of Robert Fiddler as he hears the cruel words of Christianity directed through this missionary from an alien force somewhere beyond forests. Adoption of Christianity might help the Sucker clan gain sympathy with westerners in their quest of survival. Treaties too, might help. When it became clear that a treaty would be signed at Island Lake, discussions took place among the clans over long portage in the Bay River basin at Sandy Lake, Windy Lake and Caribou Lake.

Thomas and the elder, Abraham Mamakeesik, explain how the clans reacted.

* * *

Thomas Fiddler: Before treaty Robert Fiddler went down to Berens River. The people of Berens River had a treaty already. Robert went to see an old man there every summer. This old man's name was Jacob Berens. He was a half-breed but he was Chief. At this time most of the people at Berens River were half-breeds because white men, who came down from the Bay area, had mingled with the people.

Jacob Berens taught Robert to be Chief and how to talk to the white man. One of the matters raised by Jacob Berens was the necessity of fertile land to grow crops on for the people.

Depending on the water levels, Robert Fiddler travelled either down the Crooked River to the Berens River, or down the Black Birch River to get to Berens River at the mouth of Lake Winnipeg. Robert tried to learn all he could from Jacob Berens about treaty and dealing with the white man.

* * *

I'll tell you a story that happened at the time they were going to have treaty. At this time they all said that they were going to pick one leader. They all agreed that what this person said would be the Word, and they would follow it.

There was one leader who told his people: 'make a clearing and clear the bush away to make a house.' The leader told the people to make a clearing and once it was cleared there was going to be a house built there as a store. The people believed him. Now, the people did not build that store, they just made a clearing. They thought this store would fall from the sky. They waited all summer for that store to land in that clearing. Near fall the people went back to where they would winter. Some people that left then returned to see if the store had arrived.

The people that had this leader had to watch out for what he said.

This leader even told the people that the ropes to lower the store from the sky would be red in colour.

This happened before there was a treaty over in the Island Lake area.

Before treaty there is talk of this person being Chief, or leading. I believe his English name is Joseph Linklater. At this time the families were hoping to have three settlements and a leader in every settlement for the treaty. But, they wouldn't allow three chiefs in the area.

So, Robert Fiddler, my father, took it all over at treaty.

* * *

Abraham Mamakeesik: There was a settlement at the HBC outpost on Narrows Lake and some of the people split up from there just before treaty was at Island Lake. Robert Fiddler and the Suckers went to Caribou Lake, Sandy Mamakeesik and family went to Caribou Lake. Charles Fiddler, Adam Fiddler, Jean Batiste Fiddler, Posagee-Johnny Goodman, James Meekis and John Rae all went to Caribou Lake.

But most of the Mamakeesiks, who are Sturgeons, went to Island Lake. That's how I have relatives over there. My father, Sandy Mamakeesik went to Caribou Lake. Sandy was raised in James Meekis' family. Sandy married Betsy Fiddler, Jack Fiddler's daughter.

There were others that didn't agree to go to Caribou Lake. Henry Fiddler and his mother went to Island Lake. Mooniyas, who was called by his people – The Black Man – took his family there. Waymeshoos – Jonah Flett – went. Andrew Flett, the oldest of the Fletts, took his family. Jacob Wood was here then moved. Loon Foot went to Island Lake.

I think there may have been several meetings before they all moved.

The people here, Fiddlers and family, have been in Sandy since the time of their memory. They hadn't moved from anywhere. They weren't going anywhere, either.

* * *

Thomas Fiddler: A lot of people in the Sandy Lake area – the Mooniyas – led by The Black Man, Johnny Mooniyas, the McDougalls, the Fletts, went to Island Lake in 1909 when there is a treaty and stayed there.

Yes, it's true about this meeting. It was in 1909, when they went to have that meeting. Even people from Cliff Dweller Lake came to that meeting. Kakagamicks, Kakapetums and Harpers also come to the meeting. When they had this meeting at the HBC outpost, only the men went. They didn't take their families. Robert Fiddler's message for Indian Affairs was that his group was going to stay at Caribou Lake and that they wanted Indian Affairs to come over to give them treaty money.

I have already told you that my father, Robert, had three wives. From the woman, Sarah, he has sons, Moses, James and Isaac. From Mindemoyay, he has a son, John and daughter, Mary. From Elizabeth Mooniyas, I was born and my brother, Alfred.

At Big Sandy, the people heard there was going to be a treaty over at Island Lake. Practically half the people from Sandy went over to Island Lake for the treaty. Even Robert Fiddler went over there. At this time, Robert had already been selected chief.

They heard that an Indian agent was going to be in Island Lake. They went over to tell him they were going to have their reserve down in Caribou Lake.

When Robert Fiddler went to Island Lake, O'jowitch and son, Henry, stayed over there. She had a sister there and she wanted to stay there.

Ever since that time, O'jowitch and Henry Fiddler stayed over there except when they came to visit, like to trap. They usually came to O'pasquiang or Big Sandy or Caribou Lake for awhile.

The Island Lake Treaty was not satisfactory for Robert Fiddler and James Meekis. This conclusion they reached early in 1909, when they had been down at the HBC post at Little Grand Rapids. It would be better to sign treaty at Little Grand they reasoned, especially in the face of hostility form the HBC manager at Island Lake. Fiddler and Meekis had a letter sent expressing their wishes.

> To: His Majesty's Officer of The Indian Department
> June 18, 1909
> From: Robert Fiddler
> We, the number of the band of Sucker Indians, Nap-may-pinisuk, formerly living at Sandy Lake but now permanently located at Caribou Lake, four days travel to the northwest desire to state as one man, we wish to be taken into Treaty at Little Grand Rapids and to receive our annual money payments and to have at this place, Caribou Lake, a suitable reserve set aside for our use as long as we live.
> Furthermore, we desire that this Reserve include adjoin or surround the claim staked out for Mission premises by our missionary, Reverend Arthur Santmier, and we hereby petition the government to grant us school supplies and medical supplies....
> They are in our band, 23 men, 27 women, 23 boys and 19 girls, a total of 92....
> Being fully four days nearer to Little Grand than we are to Island Lake, we earnestly petition to be received at Little Grand Rapids as stated above.
> All of which is respectfully submitted:
>
> His Mark X Robert Fiddler, Chief
> His Mark X James Bead (Meekis), Counsellor
> His Mark X Arthur Anke Flatstone, Counsellor at
>   Little Grand
> John R. Moar HBC Trader. Interpreter
> Per Arthur Santmier[39]

On August 12, 1909, Robert Fiddler and James Meekis were at Island Lake to watch the treaty being signed. Here a treaty document was signed under questionable conditions. One hundred and six people from a population of just over three hundred have 'influenza.' The doctor in the treaty party calls it 'a serious epidemic of La Grippe.' According to the Indian Agent, John Semmens, 'accompanying the illness is a condition of poverty and destitution, which is impossible to describe.'

On the day of Treaty, all of the sick and starving people rise in the hope that treaty will make their lives better in the forest. 'All the Island Lake people and the Sandy Lake people rose to their feet as one and declared for Treaty.' Not all the hunters rise. 'Nine Men Heads Of Families,' hailing from Caribou Lake refuse to accept Treaty at this point. Remaining seated in the crowd are Robert Fiddler, Adam Fiddler, Joseph Linklater, James Meekis, William Meekis, Charles Goodman, Henry Linklater, Kakagamick and Kakapetum of the Bay River district.

Semmens urges these hunters of the Sucker people to sign the Island Lake Treaty. They refuse to sign a treaty away from their ancestral grounds. A year later, on May 28, 1910, John Semmens of the Indian Department with twelve others leave Berens River to journey to Caribou Lake in the Bay River forests. They travel due east up the Berens River. Then, canoes turn northward and ten days later cross the height of land by going up a high hill with steep rocky sides. They go down the portages into the ancestral rivers and lakes of Sucker, Pelican and Crane clans. At noon the next day, the arrive at 'a space on the river bank, cleared and surrounded with a partial fence.' Leader Robert Fiddler and his hunters greet Semmens and the Treaty Party.

At 1:00 by a time piece, John Semmens, through an interpreter speaks to the Sucker people. 'Not a single person speaks English,' among the clan folk.

Then Semmens explains to the Sucker people, 'precisely as if they were children' that he gives greetings and goodwill from the King, who wishes them well. The King wants to see them, 'improve their position.'

Explaining the treaty 'in simple language' Semmens says that 'they would give up' their right to the land. In exchange, they would be paid five dollars a head per annum as long as the sun shone. The King would give them a reserve which would become their property. At treaty time each year, the King would give them all a free meal and leave a supply of bacon, flour and tea with the Chief for destitute members of the band. Each year, the King is to give a quantity of fishing tackle, powder and shot. A school for their children will be maintained. The clans will be supplied with carpenters' tools. Upon taking agriculture, seed and implements, oxen and cows would be given to them. The 'Chief' will receive a salary of twenty five dollars a year. All this is said to the clansmen who sit on the ground listening. The women and children sit a distance away.

Semmens then asks those willing to go into treaty to stand up. A newspaper reporter in the party describes the reaction: 'Slowly and phlegmatically, as if it were difficult to overcome innate pride, the whole band eventually stood up.'[40]

The twelve men, twenty-six women, thirty-six boys and twenty-one girls of the Sucker people, unknowingly relinquish their ancestral ground for a down payment of $970.

The discussion for this treaty lasted exactly one hour.

The amount of forest ceded is approximately 12,000 square miles.

Treaty for the Suckers is a confusing thing. The white men ask the ages of the people, but the people never think of how old they are, they think of how well they are. Some people just guessed at their ages and this was a disadvantage for many in later life. The Treaty – the only thing about the treaty was the white men began to share a little but the treaty also took more away.

* * *

Thomas Fiddler: At the treaty at Caribou Lake, James Meekis Big Trap, was chosen as counsellor. At this time, the people did not consider moving all the families of people together. So, in Sandy Lake, another leader was elected, a man named Peter

Kakekagamick was chosen. Elizah Kakekagamick was chosen as his counsellor. Elizah's father and Peter were brothers. At Cliff Dweller Lake, Joseph Linklater was selected leader and Adam Rae was his counsellor. All of these men were sub-chiefs to Robert Fiddler.

* * *

Treaty or not, life for the Sucker and Pelican clan folk in the Bay River forests was difficult. Treaty supplies and tools were a boom to survival. Still, there was always the long winter to face. The availability of fish, rabbits and moose was important for food supplies. Often these creatures were not found and hunger gnawed on people's stomachs.

* * *

Thomas Fiddler: I was born about October 15th, 1904, south of Big Sandy Lake, at a smaller lake near Windy Lake called Bear Head Lake. My father is Robert Fiddler, oldest son of Jack Fiddler, who is the son of Porcupine Standing Sideways. My father, Robert Fiddler, had two wives: Elizabeth who was the wife of Enos Loon Foot and Margaret. Margaret is my mother. I have four older brothers and one older sister and a younger brother, Alfred.

During the 1900s we never had flour to cook bannock. In fact, we did not have any of the white man's food: tea, flour, sugar, or bacon. Sometimes it was a hard life for the people because the winter was bitter cold. When it is coldest, rabbits will not snare because they would eat the snare string. It is seldom we catch them. Often the people make fish hooks and set through the ice but it is hard to catch fish also.

I am hungry much of the time.

In these days life is very hard: we use rabbit skins for trousers and coats. When we are very hungry, we try to find old camping sites where old bones could be found to gnaw on. We have to survive. One winter food is so scare, one of William Mamakeesik's wives and all her children starved to death on Big Sandy Lake.

Chief Jacob Berens and Wife, Berens River Landing, 1909.
Courtesy, United Church Archives, Toronto.

In 1909, Robert Fiddler spent several days with Jacob at Berens River Landing to learn about the nature of treaties.

Berens himself was a man of fantastic physical strength and endurance. It is reported he sailed a skiff across Lake Winnipeg and back to Berens River in 16 hours. Berens also worked as a dispatch runner between Norway House at St. Paul, Minnesota. Jacob Berens was the fastest man in the employ of the Hudson's Bay Company at this time.

Our family is starving too: my father, Robert Fiddler, brought seven rabbits home. But father has two wives and there are seven of us children. In order to feed the whole family, the women cooked the rabbits whole; we ate hair, guts and all. We had to, even though it tastes bad. This winter we ate black stuff off the rocks, wakwun. The women collected it, boiled it to soften it. Then we ate it. We caught a few rabbits in dead falls by setting string, which the rabbits ate, setting off a log which fell and crushed them.

The woman used to fish when I was a small boy. If they didn't catch fish we didn't eat because there was no flour in these days. We were starving and couldn't feed our dogs and they starved so we ate them to live.

One time at Caribou Lake when we were very hungry, I recall my father, Robert, had a 44 calibre gun. That gun used to hold ten bullets. My father and my older brothers and uncles, Moses, James, Charles and Jean Batiste went out hunting in the Windy Lake area. When they were out hunting this time, they discovered that other people had been there and built a mutikwan. Because they found this wooden structure, that's where they made camp.

At this time our people had no dogs for hauling. From this camp my father, Robert, killed several moose by himself and the rest of the hunters didn't get any. They did not cut all the moose up. They hid most of them in the snows. My brothers hauled some of the meat back to the mutikwan, their camp. After they finished preparing everything, they headed back home toward Caribou Lake with some of the meat. They arrived there about midnight.

All the people got up and started working and everybody feasted in the middle of the night. After everyone had eaten, they started packing. They had to carry all their belongings on their backs or on toboggans. We left that night and we walked all day and the next day to get to Windy Lake. It was late in the evening when we arrived. (We walked about sixty miles.) We stayed at this place on the south shore for about a month. The people prepared all the food and fats. We left this place around March and moved across country to Big Beaver Lake.

When we arrived on Big Beaver Lake we had to build a

brand new camp. The people used birchbark for coverings on their huts because there was no canvas at this time. On Big Beaver Lake my father killed lots of caribou. Sometimes he used to kill about ten a day. That meat was all prepared by drying it up.

When it was getting later in the spring – there is only bare ice on the lakes – we moved to another place on the river down from Two Beach Lake. When we arrived at that river, it was open. Our canoes weren't there, they were down on Caribou Lake. When the water wasn't rising up, we walked along the river edge to get down to Caribou Lake. At the end of the last rapids, the men went on ahead to get the canoes.

Then we stayed on Caribou Lake and the men made some more canoes. If one person wanted a canoe, all the men would help him with it until it was finished. They all worked on one canoe before they started another one. All they used to make the canoe were curved knives. The women used to sew up the birchbark with roots. The men did the carving. This way a lot of canoes could be made in a short time.

During this time the people helped each other a lot. When a hunter kills a moose, they divide it equally among the people. The hunter who killed the moose does not expect any payment. Even if one person kills a beaver, the woman would cut up the meat and divide it among the people, everyone getting the same share.

During this time when they met up with a white man they used to respect the white man quite a bit. It doesn't happen this way anymore.

* * *

I am going to tell you a story when I was a boy, when I didn't know how to trap. I was out constantly with trappers like Thompson Quill (the son of Joseph Fiddler). There was one thing I saw Thompson do when he was trapping foxes. A long time ago, we just used traps for foxes. We didn't use snares.

When the snow is getting deep along the rivers and lakes – Thompson was the only one I saw trapping foxes like this; he got a six foot pole. When he saw fox tracks on the lake, he dug out the snow and lay down the pole to secure his trap. To place his trap, he dug another hole to put it in.

For the trap, he got rabbit's fur. He trimmed off the long hairs, then he cut it into round pieces about the size of the trap trigger. Of course, he had his weejana. The rabbit fur froze on the trigger so it would not come off. Then, he covered it up with about three feet of snow. Whenever a fox came around, it smelled the trap under the snow and started digging until it reached the bait.

I was out constantly with trappers. I watched them when they were setting up their snares and when they were making their wooden traps. They were using wooden traps and snares for lynx. I watched and learned how to snare a lynx. Of course, everyone knows how a curious lynx will follow human tracks.

There were no wire snares, a twine was used.

Well, Thompson Quill told me to go out and make a wooden trap for him. He also gave me a snare for an animal. It took me the whole day to make the wooden trap – you look for a place with lots of trees close together.

We put up snares where a lynx or a fisher often passes through. To set the snare, I followed my tracks back from the wooden trap. Then, I put a pole across the trail and put the snare there.

I was about ten years old and hadn't killed any animals yet.

The next morning, it had snowed a little bit, but the trail was visible when I went to check the sets. I was getting close to the snare when I saw fresh lynx tracks heading straight for my snare. When I saw those tracks, I started hoping and praying I would catch it. When I reached the place, I didn't see the pole I placed across the path for my snare. The two sticks for the snare were knocked aside. There were tracks all over the place.

I saw the pole quite a way off. There was nothing there but it. When I walked up to the pole, I saw the lynx had chewed itself free. I knelt there and started crying. After I got tired of crying, I went home.

* * *

We travelled all over when I was a child. I recall one fall we went to Cliff Dweller Lake, where the river is; a group of us

Chief Robert Fiddler, 1910..br Photo, A. Vernon Thomas.
Courtesy, Manitoba Archives.

went over there to spend the winter at the rapids. The people that were there at that time were: Robert Fiddler, Thompson Quill, Adam Fiddler, William Goodman, Jean Baptiste Fiddler, Jerry Fiddler, Frances Meekis – many were there – lots of children.[41]

At this rapids, if you go up the river where the waters come from, there were lots of good whitefish spawning.

Everyone knew that cold weather was coming. When we got to that rapids we cut down big trees and made a dam right across the rapids. Water would go through the dam but the fish could not go through. At the top of the dam, water came over on log slides down to square log bins that held the fish when they came over.

Sometimes when the fish got stuck on the slide an owl would land on a dry spot but of course it got sprinkled with water and got wet. It sat there cold and freezing. It wouldn't fly away, it was frozen where it was sitting.

At this place we killed as many whitefish as we could. The women usually took the guts out of the fish and roasted the fish over the fire. When they finished roasting them they set them up and they got hard. After that they just grinded them up.

They did not throw the guts away; they boiled them to obtain grease and oil. Sometimes we caught Northern pike and inside of them there is a stomach and we blew in it to make it bigger and then left it to dry. When you blow it up and when it dries, it just stays like that. That is where we kept our fish oil.

We usually made birchbark boxes. A layer of whole fish was placed on the bottom, then covered with ground fish, then a layer of whole fish and so on.

After they filled it up they put a layer of sticks on top to really get it tight, then they poured oil on top then more powdered fish and then they closed it up.

After they finished collecting the food they took it down to Caribou Lake where there is a rocky island. The dried food was stored in a hole on that island. The hole was covered with moss and birchbark.

We knew pretty well we could hunt our own food right up until Christmas before the real cold weather set in. After this we could not hunt very much. In January and February it was too cold for any hunter to get anything. This was when we used our supply of stored food to live.

In those early days there were no white man or white missionaries around. Nor did we have any white man's medicine or know that doctors even existed. But even when it was in the coldest time of the winter we shovelled out snow, laid branches and built a small fire for our women to have their babies. One woman, Mrs. Emily Kakegamik of Caribou Lake, who had her child this way, is still alive. I mention this to show that Indians survived without the help of any white men.

There were many things the Indian people did to survive in the days of my father, Robert Fiddler, and his father, Jack Fiddler.

**

The first Hudson's Bay trading post came to Caribou Lake around 1910. That was when we were introduced to white man's food. I didn't like the taste of butter. It stunk as far as I was concerned. Many people did not like canned meat either. When I ate a can I got sick and vomited.

I recall it was in the fall that we went on a memorable hunt. We started out from Caribou Lake and headed east toward Cliff Dweller Lake. Four of us took two large canoes, one would hold eight hundred pounds, the other, seven hundred. We paddled away and just before dark that night we killed a loon. It was the only game we saw all that day. We cooked it and drank the water it was boiled in. The next morning we had nothing to eat.

We paddled out again to hunt moose and it started to rain heavily but we kept going. It rained all that day and we did not have anything to eat. Nor did we have a tent for shelter so we stood under a thick branched tree for protection. We only had tea and a little bit of tobacco that day. The next day it was still raining.

We did not move out from under the trees that day. Toward the end of the second day it started to snow. Soon the ground was covered with a foot and one half of snow. We were a long way from home and the second day ended and we still had not eaten.

The next day we portaged by the falls and went into Two Beach Lake and kept going; portaging by two more falls. The snow in the portage trails was deep and it was hard walking. All of us were in one canoe because we had left the other one behind at the first portage.

My uncle, Charley Fiddler, was one of the men in our party and he was very old in years. Annie Kakegamik was on the hunt too. I was in the youth of life but Thompson Quill, the other member of our group, was handicapped. His legs were paralyzed and he crawled to get along on the portages.

We still kept hunting for moose but we could not find any; not even tracks were to be seen in the snow. Later that day when the skies started to clear we made camp. Three days had passed since we had eaten.

I picked up some string and went out into the bush to set some rabbit snares but there were not any tracks in the fresh snow so I wasn't very hopeful. The next morning my uncle Charley woke me up and asked me to go out and check my snares. He said there were a lot of rabbit tracks around our camp. I started out slowly because I could hardly walk from lack of food.

I managed to walk by stumbling from one tree to another. When I came to my first snare, the rabbits had eaten the string I had used. At the second snare, a rabbit had been caught but it had broken away. I felt real depressed when I saw that. I went to the third snare and I saw a rabbit was caught. Just seeing the rabbit gave me enough strength to return to the camp. The four of us ate the rabbit, fur and all.

The next day I killed a squirrel and a muskrat and we ate but we were still all very weak. I went out again that same morning, looking for partridge. I came upon a flock of them and killed twenty with my old muzzle loader. On my way back to the camp, I shot a rabbit. Between the four of us we ate the twenty partridge and the rabbit.

Then after the meal we all felt much stronger so we set out again and portaged by more falls. After we crossed a big lake I

Women of the Caribou Lake Band, 1910.
Photo, A. Vernon Thomas. Courtesy, Manitoba Archives.

killed three more partridges and ate some more. At the end of the day, the lame man, Thompson Quill, killed a moose. We were all very happy that we had lots to eat the next morning.

Then our luck changed, we killed three more moose before we left that camp on White Island Lake. We had so much meat we could not carry it all in one canoe thus it was necessary to make several return trips bringing the moose meat out to the second canoe. But on the way back we shot another moose; then we had five moose. Finally, we all got home with all the meat. We went from starving to a feast that time.

* * *

The clan hunters did not alway kill moose with guns for each hunter did not own one. Often, three or four men shared a single, treasured firearm. Moose were commonly run down in the deep snows and speared in the days of Robert Fiddler. In the 1920s and 30s, use of the long bow was still practised in the forests. The bows were hand carved from birch, the arrows were blunt-ended and killed by impact. Hunters brought home bags of rabbits, partridge and squirrels with the ancient weapon. Even steel traps were not all that common but wire had replaced string for rabbit, fox and bear snares.

All families trapped, or worked as outpost traders or transported supplies for the HBC. Thomas Fiddler worked for part of his time with the Hudson's Bay Company. This story happened east of Caribou Lake and is an illustration that carelessness in the forest exacts a deadly price.

* * *

Thomas Fiddler: This incident happened during the month of May, 1921. The people were all out on the trap lines with their families. There were many people trapping at this time and up in the Bay River; families came from Island Lake to Sandy Lake to trap.

There is only one trading post at this time, the HBC in Caribou Lake. In Duck Lake, Elias Rae did the trading for the HBC.

Men of the Caribou Band, 1910.
Photo, A. Vernon Thomas. Courtesy, Manitoba Archives.

This portrait of the Caribou Lake men was taken in 1910 when they signed treaty with the Dominion of Canada. 'They were,' a man a Berens River said, 'unusually large men, strong built, mostly six feet or more in height. When they came into Berens River in the Yorkboats from the north they were feared and respected by the Indians in our area who were smaller in stature.'

The men in this picture are: front row starting from the second man on the left – Charles Goodman, Charlie Fiddler, James Meekis, 'Kitchi Wah-nee-gin,' Adam Fiddler, Abraham Meekis, William Meekis, Alfred Meekis, Moses Mamageesik. The man on the far right is unidentified.

In Sandy Lake, William Goodman traded for the HBC. In Northwind Lake, my uncle, Charles Fiddler, did the trading for the HBC.

As for me, the HBC hires me to go from settlement to settlement to pick up the furs. We go, paddles and canoes, for there are no motors yet. My brother, Alfred, is with me and we travel with four others: Fred Moar, Peter Crowe, Titus Goodman and Jake Meekis.

We went to Duck Lake first to pick up the furs plus what was left of the HBC trade goods. Then we went to Northwind Lake. At Northwind we parted with the other four, we were going the other direction back to Caribou Lake. Their destination was to go down to Sandy Lake then back to the Caribou Lake HBC store.

When Alfred and I parted with them in the afternoon, Northwind Lake was so calm. Those four stayed and hunted for bear on Northwind Lake. They bedded down there for the night.

Alfred and I slept down on the river.

Early in the morning, before we got up, the wind was already blowing hard.

Fred Moar, Jake Meekis, Titus and Peter Crowe went on their way that morning. They portaged up in to the Trout Lakes. Now, in Trout Lakes there is one island where the seagulls lay their eggs. They went to that island to gather some eggs. Everyone jumped out of the canoe without even making certain the canoe is secure.

They were busy gathering eggs. Suddenly, they saw their canoe being carried by the wind, drifting it on the lake. Jake Meekis jumped into the water and swam after the canoe. Jake caught up with the canoe and tried to tow the canoe back to the island. Jake was holding on to the canoe in the middle. The wind was blowing hard, waves splashed against the canoe and landed on Jake's head. With all the water landing on his head, Jake finally let go of the canoe and drowned.

The others were afraid to go after the canoe. One of them had already drowned for going after it.

In the early spring it happens most times that it will rain and snow as well. So, Titus Goodman, Fred Moar and Peter Crowe

James Fiddler at Caribou Lake. Collection, Thomas Fiddler.

were soaked and wet. They froze when it snowed and they had nothing to eat after the seagull eggs were gone. For twelve days they stayed on that small island.

People from Sandy Lake came to Caribou Lake, asking why no one had come to pick up their furs. This was how we discovered something had happened to the four. They were supposed to go to Sandy Lake, too.

The people from Sandy Lake went right back that night. They told the rest of the people that the crew left Northwind eleven days ago to go to Trout and Sandy. Three canoes left Sandy Lake to start the search.

I came the other way to Northwind Lake with three canoes to join the search. We brought materials used for funerals, black silk and lumber. But, we didn't know what to expect, we carried it just in case. When we arrived at Trout Lake we found the people from Sandy Lake with the remainder of the crew. The three men were barely alive. They could not drink nor swallow anything. The only thing we gave them was a little milk. For three days, we stayed in this place before we were able to feed them and move them back to Sandy Lake.

Today Fred Moar is still alive in Little Grand Rapids. Titus is well in Sandy Lake.

* * *

Thomas Fiddler mentioned that he saw his first airplane in 1925, the flying box that his grandfather Jack, had seen years previously in visions. Airplanes were to have little benefit to clansmen at this time because their use was limited to government activity and prospecting ventures. But a western machine that would take much labor out of forest living was soon to arrive and it would be Thomas who owned the first of these among the Sucker clan.

* * *

Thomas Fiddler: In 1925, coming up from Little Grand Rapids, we first saw an outboard motor. One of the prospectors was using a Johnson three horse.

We were in our canoe near Caribou Lake. I was with my

Clara Jesmer, Fannie Meekis, Cecelia, Betsy, Sen, Emma, Wosies Meekis, Jodus Meekis. All but Clara and Cecelia died in their teens or early twenties from T.B. Photo, Jean Lindokken, 1938.

brother Alfred Fiddler, and we heard this sound coming. As soon as we came around the shore bend, we saw the prospectors in one canoe, pulling two canoe loads of supplies. We stopped paddling. We could see these guys just sitting in their canoe, doing nothing.

This lake we were on was about a five mile stretch and we just watched them in amazement until they passed right out of sight.

When we got to Caribou Lake, we took off our freight and we paddled to the bay where we were camped.

Alfred couldn't get that outboard motor out of his mind. He said out loud: 'I wonder if I'll never get a boat with a motor on it in my lifetime.'

That fall, we came down to Windy Lake to spend the winter. All the people moved this way to Windy Lake but I had to go back because I trapped way southwest near Poplar River. During the winter while I trapped I never forgot that motor. How much I wanted to own one. During that winter I collected my pelts and saved them up. I was aiming to get that motor.

In the springtime I didn't go back to my trap line. I stayed around Windy Lake and trapped muskrats. I was going to go down to Berens River. I was determined to get a motor. I already had the pelts to do it.

After I told Mr. Patterson at Caribou Lake HBC store what I was to do, he asked me if he could see my pelts. I told Mr. Patterson: 'There's no reason to prevent you from seeing them. You can see them if you want to.'

After Mr. Patterson saw my pelts he asked if I would buy the motor from the HBC. Mr. Patterson took the pelts. The motor had to come in by boat freight.

I was going down to Berens River. Before I left, I asked Mr. Patterson for some money because I wanted to rent a motor coming back from Berens River; the Berens River people had motors. Mr. Patterson gave me fifty dollars.

The Berens River people knew me these days.

The first person I saw in Berens River, I asked him if I could rent his motor. This person agreed to lend me his motor.

Immediately, I began the trip back – driving. I didn't work at all. I just sat there. The portages were nothing.

The rent for the motor was thirty dollars.

When I got back, my new motor was waiting for me. Since 1926, I've had an outboard motor.

* * *

After 1925, many new elements of western progress would appear in the boreal forests of the clansmen. These elements would be the Ministry of Lands and Forests of Ontario, private prospectors, the police, and the incursion of western medicine practises. In the midst of these years, several changes would occur for the Sucker clansmen. Most startling would be Robert Fiddler's decision to lead the Sucker clan away from Caribou Lake where the treaty had been implemented sixteen years before.

Robert Fiddler's decision to lead the Sucker clan away from Caribou and Windy Lake in 1925-26 was prefaced by a tragic event, the loss of his son, James. For a number of years, James was a labourer at the HBC Caribou Lake post. A written report of this event is held on the pages of Adam Fiddler's Syllabic book. Under May 12, 1926, the syllabics read.

> It was this day they found the body of James Fiddler. These were James Fiddler's belongings: '1 quilt, 11 pants, 2 suits, 3 hats, pocket watch, shotgun & shells, moccasins, 3 long coats, 2 sweaters, checkers and board, 1 pipe, harmonica, gun powder, gun flints, etc.'[42]

Thomas says that, James Fiddler was considered a very wealthy man, for it is unlikely that any other person in the clan had the equal in material goods that were possessed by James. The death of James Fiddler was unusual in its nature and caused his father, Robert, much sorrow. Stories circulated concerning James' demise and Edward Rae relates how some people see his death.

* * *

Edward Rae: There's a little lake just over the hill here at Caribou Lake. This little lake is called Woman's Lake because this was once a burnt area and the ladies used to go and pick berries by that lake. That's how it got the name Woman's Lake.

One time, a man, James Fiddler, the leader's son, drowned in this lake and they searched in the lake for two weeks without finding anything. Adam Fiddler was helping look for this body too but they couldn't find it even though that lake is very shallow. The lake is real shallow and weedy and they just couldn't find anything.

This man who drowned, James Fiddler, Robert Fiddler's son, was a fully grown man. He could have been married but he wasn't. James Fiddler had been working at the HBC store since the time he was real young. I heard this James was bothering Fred Moar's wife and apparently Fred Moar asked an old man over in Little Grand Rapids to do something about it. This old man was called O'kahneeg. O'kahneeg was blamed for this drowning. The way the people figured it, Matchi-Manitou, the devil was taking James Fiddler around and that was why he drowned and that was why they couldn't find the body either. The devil took him.

I was a young man when this happened, maybe eighteen, and the older men would not let any of us young men go up to the Lake to help drag for the body.

After the men on Woman's Lake had searched for a long time, and done everything they could and failed, Adam Fiddler called all the men together. He instructed all the men to take their canoes to the middle of the lake and form a circle. They did that and Adam prayed and asked Manitou to show them where this body was. After Adam prayed they just started going one way or another dragging for the body and soon they found it.

This was just one of the things that Adam Fiddler performed.

* * *

James Fiddler's death was not the reason his father decided to lead the Sucker clan away from Caribou Lake. Ecological considerations ranked foremost. Food for the Sucker clan's survival was an important consideration. Beside this, Caribou

Lake had never been officially designated as a reserve ground, although a so-called treaty had been entered sixteen years before. Thomas Fiddler speculates on Robert Fiddler's reasons for the Sucker clan's migration down the Bay River to settle at the narrows between Big Sandy Lake and Narrows Lake in 1926.

* * *

Thomas Fiddler: There were people living at Sandy Lake when they had the first treaty down in the Island Lake area. From Sandy, when the treaty was approaching, they all went down to Island Lake. Some of them came back; half of them stayed down in the Island Lake area.

Robert Fiddler went down to the Island Lake area and the Indian agent who was looking after this told him to pick up the money over there but he didn't take it. He told this guy he wanted him to come down to Caribou Lake and give him that money.

The next year, in 1910, they came down to Caribou Lake to have treaty.

But in Caribou Lake, it's all rock, there was no place at all to plant even a small garden. Even if you looked around that area you couldn't find a long stretch. It's all jagged rocks.

During that time when we stayed over there – about 16 years – my father began to think about staying and making it their reserve.

Pretty soon they began to talk about moving to another location. The people knew the land in the Sandy Lake area and they decided to move there. I believe my father probably liked it there and when Robert first said that we would move to Sandy Lake, I was very disappointed inside myself but I never said that to my father.

In 1926, my father, Robert, myself, and Monias Fiddler, came over to Sandy Lake to look over the land. We had a pick with us, when we came to the river we went ashore to see how fertile the land was. It appeared the land was fertile.

After this summer we came over to check Sandy Lake, the people moved up to Windy Lake in the fall.

James Meekis, Big Trap, didn't want to leave Caribou Lake area; he was dead set against it so he stayed. From all his sons, Sandy Mamakeesik, and Alfred Meekis, were the only two that came along with us.

When we first came down to the Windy Lake area, we stayed there for two winters and we went down to Caribou Lake for treaties.

Robert Fiddler and some people came by the Bay River to Sandy. He brought down seeds for a garden and in those two summers he planted prosperous gardens there.

Another group of us came around the other way, in the Windy Lake direction down through Trout Lake – through there.

The people who were already at east Sandy Lake were the Kakapetums and the Kakapetums and the Kakekagamics and Harpers.

It was about 1928 when we came to Sandy and chose it as the reserve.

* * *

During the migration to Sandy Lake the Sucker clan members discovered that prospectors were roaming the forests near Windy and Northwind Lakes. Thomas Fiddler worked for some of these prospectors, hauling supplies with his dog team.

With prospectors roaming in the Sucker clansmen's forests, staking claims, it became imperative for Robert Fiddler to select a site for a reserve and he and the people decide that the grounds between Sandy and Narrows Lake will be their location. In 1929, Treaty Commissioners, Cain and Awrey, flew into Big Sandy Lake to talk to Robert Fiddler about the granting of reserve lands. Cain and Awrey find Robert Fiddler, clan leader. They describe him as the, 'striking looking Chief Fiddler, arrayed in his official uniform with his large medal bearing the impression of the late Edward VII.'

It is decided at this meeting that three hundred and thirty two of the clansmen will get 17 square miles of ground 'laid out in a rectangle having a width of at least 3 miles....' The reserve that Robert Fiddler has selected has reduced the

Chief Robert Fiddler, 1937. Photo, J. Satterly.
Courtesy, Ontario Department of Mines.

upland country of his ancestors from 12,000 square miles of mother earth to seventeen.[43]

It will be another sixteen years before this selected ground becomes an official reserve, mainly because of the Province of Ontario's insistence that native clansmen should not gain any ground that has an economic resource in it or on it.

The movement of the Sucker clan to Sandy Lake meant that the days of operation of the HBC post at Caribou Lake were numbered. Only the Meekis families of the Pelican clan, Raes of the Sturgeon clan and Thompson Quill, a single Sucker clansman remained there. The bulk of the population was now settled for their summers at Sandy Lake. Soon the treaties would be held at Sandy.

Another event occurred among the clans in the early thirties, a white woman and white man came to live permanently among the Pelican clansmen on Bay River at Caribou Lake. The man was a Norwegian, Oscar Lindokken and his wife Jean was a nurse, who was raised on a farm near Woodstock, Ontario. In these days, Jean Lindokken often gives out the benefits of western medicine because she is appalled by the poor health of the clansmen. Tuberculosis is a rampant disease and the clansmen who live in large communal structures for both protection and pleasure easily infect each other with this contagious disease. She argues with the clansmen that they should build separate quarters for each family for the prevalence of influenza, measles, and small pox prey on groups. To her suggestions, the clansmen adjust slowly and cautiously. It will be in the fifties before communal housing is totally abandoned.

Oscar Lindokken makes his living trapping in areas where the clansmen do not frequent. With benevolence, they allow him space. Lindokken is a source of great amusement for the clansmen because of his wild humour. Native clansmen, out checking their rabbit snares in the forest, often find that somehow a large northern pike is secured in a snare. Oscar's pranks gain for him a native name and he becomes known as the Wolverine. In talking about Oscar's arrival among the people, Thomas Fiddler says: 'I want to tell you two stories about the white men. These stories are true. Almost anybody at

Sandy Lake could tell you these stories. One story is about how the Indians treated a white man and how a white man treated the Indians. The second story is how the white man treated an Indian and how an Indian treated a white man.'

* * *

Thomas Fiddler: This is a story about Oscar Lindokken, the white man, the people call the Wolverine. When he first came here he was trapping around the Windy Lake area. At that time he didn't have anything except what he carried on his back but he was young and very strong.

After he was at Windy Lake, he came down to Sandy Lake to trap. He made his camp at the exit of Big Sandy Lake. There were also some of the people living around there at that time.

In the fall, Sandy Lake and the Bay River froze over. It was very cold. That morning when Oscar got up, he went to the edge of the river and tested the ice. It was very solid and he thought he could get across the lake without any trouble. He was anxious to get off trapping. He packed his bag and started out. When he reached the place where the current was swift, he fell through the ice.

The people saw him fall through but he was quite away from them. They got a canoe to try and get him out.

It was very, very cold.

By the time they reached him he was almost drowned and they hauled him inside the boat. They took Oscar back to their lodging place to revive him because he was half-drowned and half-dead. Inside the lodgings, they took all of his wet clothes off. They rolled him up in a blanket. Oscar didn't recover for a long time – until his strength came back.

At this time Oscar wasn't poor. He knew that he had almost drowned and that the Indians had saved him from drowning. He also knew he would pay a debt to these people for saving his life. Oscar knew he would try to help the Indian people every year.

When Oscar finished trapping, he started selling supplies at Caribou Lake. As soon as he was able to get an airplane of his own, he did so. The money for that airplane came from the

Indian people themselves. Oscar knew this and it is probably why he stays among the Indian people, as long as he lives.

As far as I knew and as far I've seen, Oscar has tried to help the Indian people as much as he can. For example, when Oscar had a store in Caribou Lake all the people had snow machines. Ateyen Kakagamick said that of all those snow machines, no one has paid for them yet.

Ateyen told me, 'I paid forty dollars for my skidoo and I probably paid the most.'

When Oscar was very active in working I was also very active. We liked each other. We were buddies together.

I'm very thankful to Oscar and his wife, Jean, for all they have done for my people in the past.

**

This next story comes from Sandy Lake. I don't know the exact year, possibly 1932. During this time, no one had a store at Big Sandy but there was a small outpost. The big HBC store was in Caribou Lake.

The Indian people were scattered all over trapping.

There was one Indian from Sandy Lake working for the outpost which was run by two white men. This Indian man was taking groceries around to different camps and collecting furs. His name was Jimmy Kakekugamick and his wife's name was Eva. She was a daughter of Charley Fiddler.

When Jimmy was working for the outpost, the white man always stayed behind with Jimmy's wife.

It was during the time the people were living at the river out of Narrows Lake. It was in the springtime when the two white men came with Jimmy and his wife to hunt ducks. They were staying at the river also, living in tents. Everybody lived in tents in the spring and summer at this time.

These white men were named Alex Gunn and Bill Dossey. They asked Jimmy if he would go out overnight duck hunting so one of them could have his woman.

About the time I realized what was going on, not only me but the whole village knew about it.

At this time, Jimmy's mind was going because of what these

Alfred Sterling, 1933. Photo, Jean Lindokken.

two white men were doing. At this time, the white men were mistreating Jimmy. Jimmy thought to himself, he would mistreat them, too. When the white men went off to Caribou Lake, Jimmy went into the outpost store and took grocery goods. When the white men returned they knew right away someone had broken into the store and stolen goods.

These two white men tried to find out who did this.

While the white men were away, the people knew for a fact, that the only person who went to the outpost was Jimmy.

These two white men informed the soldiers* at Berens River. The two soldiers came in by dog team to pick up Jimmy.

At this time my father, Robert, was chief.

Jimmy was living at the river and the two white men that reported him never came to the river. Only the soldiers with a paper about their complaint came to the river.

I was there when a soldier talked to Jimmy.

The soldier told Jimmy: 'We received a note of complaint that you broke into a store and took supplies.'

Jimmy didn't say a word.

The soldier told Jimmy: 'If you really did this – tell me – if you tell me – I will help you all I can.'

When Jimmy heard the soldier say they were going to help him, he immediately told them he was the one that broke into the store.

The soldier asked Jimmy what was on his mind when he took the supplies.

Jimmy said he went over to the outpost store where he was living by himself. He didn't take his wife. She was at their camp at the river. When he was walking away from the store, he thought he wanted to go right back to the river. But, he turned and went back to the store and broke in.

The soldier asked Jimmy: 'When you broke the lock to the building what was on your mind? Was there a different feeling inside of you?'

Jimmy said: 'My mind was sort of dizzy and I didn't quite know what I was doing. My mind was very upset.'

*R.C.M.P.

157

The soldier told Jimmy he would take him out of Berens River so he wouldn't do these things anymore.

I always get angry about this because these two soldiers never really tried to find out what happened.

While Jimmy was in prison he got sick from loneliness. They took him to Berens River by steam boat because they knew he was awfully sick. He never made it home. He died at Berens River.

*　*　*

The manager of the Caribou Lake HBC post in 1932 was a Scot, A.W. Gunn. Gunn wrote in his journal of this episode that, 'Jimmy has confessed as he says his sins have been troubling him but he pleads insanity.' But, Robert Fiddler tells Gunn pointedly that Jimmy was a 'good boy' until he started working for the Company.

At Caribou Lake in 1932, James Meekis, clan leader of the Pelican passes to the beyond. Adam Meekis inherits the hereditary role as clan leader and Francis Meekis assumes James' counsellor role to Robert Fiddler.

In the following year 1933, the activities of the clansmen, including Robert Fiddler, are recorded by the HBC manager, William Hendry.

June 6, 1933: 'Thomas Fiddler in from Long Narrows on his way to Berens River. Gave Thomas permission to bring one of our new square stern canoes up with freight.'

June 10, 1933: 'Counsellor Francis Meekis in today with three canoes on his way to Indian Department for supplies.'

June 23, 1933: 'Thomas Fiddler arrived today with a small load of freight.'

June 27, 1933: 'Thomson Quill came over in the forenoon and started cutting the grass around the post.'

July 24, 1933: 'Kitchi Adam Fiddler the preacher from Long Narrows arrived in today with his retinue of law makers.'

July 25, 1933: 'Robert Fiddler, the chief, arrived here today. He left with 40 men and 14 canoes for Little Grand in order to get Indian Department supplies.'

Sept. 4, 1933: 'All the children in the Meekis camp are ill. An epidemic of sickness broke out amongst them a few days ago, and to date all the children are down with it.'[44]

The new manager at the Caribou Lake HBC post is not a man who is remembered in warm words. William Hendry had been a clerk at HBC Caribou Lake in the past and he is posted there in 1933 in his first position as manager. It will be his last. Ateyin Kakagamick, an orphan in boyhood, speaks to us now of Hendry.

* * *

Ateyen Kakagamick: I went to work with the HBC when I was about fourteen. Both my parents had died then. My father died and I was raised by grandmother.

I was a messenger between Caribou Lake and the outlying posts at Sandy. Sometimes, I made more that seventy trips by snowshoes or canoe in a year. One summer, I went to Berens River five times.

When William Hendry was post manager I did not really like him. Once we went on a trip to Little Grand Rapids. At Little Grand, Mrs. Charles Moar baked a huge cake with icing on it for our journey back to Caribou Lake. All the way back to Caribou Lake, William Hendry would not share that cake with me. Hendry ate the cake one slice at a time while he watched me to see how much butter I was putting on my bannock when we had meals.

We were taking the furs out to Little Grand after the winter trapping season. All the furs from Sandy Lake, Windy Lake, Duckling Lake and Cliff Dweller Lake were delivered to Caribou Lake and then transported out to Little Grand Rapids after the trapping season was over on June 10th.

One time, William Hendry got in an open fight with Jakan Linklater, Marten's son. Hendry threw Jakan out of the post.

William Hendry, 1933. Photo, Jean Lindokken.

At Caribou Lake HBC post, William Hendry is in command. He writes in his post journal:

Sept. 8: 'Mr. and Mrs. O. Lindokken arrived here this evening on their way to Owl Lake where Lindokken is going to trap this coming winter. Owl Lake is Southeast of Caribou Lake.'

Jean Lindokken talks of the Caribou Lake HBC post.

* * *

Jean Lindokken: Oscar can tell you some of the prices these HBC traders charged. You see, they were here in Caribou Lake and the Winnipeg Office didn't know what kind of characters their men were.

I can tell you the cruelty: to see poor Thompson Quill crawling on his hands and knees. Thompson had little short legs and little tiny feet. I think he had poliomyelitis when he was a baby. It affected both his legs from the knees down. He used to get old canvas and sew it on his pant legs. He wore snow shoes strapped to his legs and dragged himself by using his hands on the front of the snowshoes.

Thompson had gotten some flour. Flour the HBC had sold; it was green and moldy and they were selling it; weighing it out and selling it over the counter to the Indians. Finally the Indians wouldn't buy it anymore so they threw it out.

And poor Thompson Quill was paralyzed from the knees down – he was a crawler. He had been out there crawling among this flour, trying to see if there wasn't something he could make use of. Then the HBC threw all the green flour in the lake so he couldn't use it. Cruel things like this are happening.

These HBC post managers were practically illiterate, they were Grade 8-9 or 7 something – low class white men. They looked on themselves as kings and the Indians were just animals. They treated Indians the way Indians treat dogs.

The prices they charged for supplies! Well, I remember at the old HBC, the cat had gone up and messed in all the brown

Thompson Quill (the Crawler), 1935.
Photo, Jean Lindokken.

sugar and the beans and stuff and they just sold it to the Indians.

The HBC Company can't be blamed for it all because everything depended on the individual post manager. In the old days the Indians could not read or write and everything was dealt with in terms of skins. In Caribou Lake, silver foxes that should have brought $150., brought $15. At tin of coffee might go to an Indian for 75 ¢ and go on the Bay books for 25 ¢ with the post manager pocketing the difference. Well, who was to know? Certainly not people in head office who might visit a post only yearly. They had no way of knowing how a post manager treated the Indians.

* * *

At Caribou Lake HBC post – William Hendry begins his last days before passing to the beyond. On Oct. 11, 1933, Hendry wrote:

> A.H. Sterling left with Moses Meekis for the Severn River where they will Fall-fish. It's rather early but better that than miss the run.
>
> Employed Elias (Rae) making six toboggans. He pulled for his Camp with the boards & the necessary tools, His camp is on the Duck Lake route.

Oct. 15, 1933: 'Busy in store all forenoon fixing up the Meekis Tribe. They departed homewards about noon.'

Oct. 15, 1933: 'Towards noon Donald and Ateyen Kakagamick pulled in from their camp. Busy in store all afternoon attending to their various wants.'

Oct. 19, 1933: 'Whitefish will soon be spawning now. Fishing was good today. The majority of Indians are now on their winter trapping grounds.'

Oct. 21 1933: 'Heavy snowfall last night. Recommenced to snow this A.M. & continued all day.'[45]

October 21st is William Hendry's last entry in the Caribou Lake HBC post journal.

When the sun settled behind the trees this winter night, Thomas and Jean Lindokken, tell us why this is Hendry's last entry.

* * *

Thomas Fiddler: It happened up in Caribou Lake. There was an HBC post at Caribou Lake. There was a manager, Mr. Hendry, and a clerk who was big and husky. These two were HBC people. These men hated James Linklater,* The Marten, because he performed the shaking tent.

These white men and the Indians could not understand each other. Jakan Linklater, Marten's son, was talking to this big husky clerk at the Caribou Lake store. They did not understand each other. The clerk threw Jakan out of the store and kicked him around.

Marten said this white man who was trying to be smart would not be able to see the man who would fight him.

These two HBC people left alone in the fall because all the people were out trapping during freeze-up.

These two HBC people had a German shepherd-type dog. It was very smart and understood what it was told but they also had five other huskies to pull sleds.

Before freeze-up, they used to set nets for dog food during the winter. In the fall they always had lots of fish to last through the winter for the dogs. These two people went to Windy Lake where there was a falls to fish. They also took all of their dogs. They lived in tents while they were fishing.

After freeze-up when people went to the store, there was no one there. I wouldn't be able to say who the first person who arrived at the post was and saw that no one was at the store. Soon the news spread that there was no HBC man or assistant and everyone knew the people were over at Windy Lake. The Indians thought they were over there fishing. They told Robert Fiddler. He said that we should start looking for the manager.

*For stories about the shamanistic abilities of James Linklater see, *Legends From The Forest*.

When they arrived at the Hudson's Bay men's Camp, they only saw the German shepherd running out on the ice from the tent. Only this dog's tracks covered the ground. These two men had disappeared. They were gone; only this dog was left. The five other dogs were gone as well.

As soon as the people realized they were gone, they went to Little Grand and brought back a Mountie. The Mountie investigated and couldn't find a clue as to what they did, where they went, or what happened.

The sleds and dog harness were gone too, but plates and food were found inside the tent. Though the dog didn't touch them because it had a lot of fish to eat.

The Mountie had lots of help from Indian people. They couldn't find a trace. Their canoes were there when they came in before freeze-up. In the spring they searched again but couldn't find a trace. We didn't know anything about what happened. At this time the white people did not know anything about how the Indians lived. If the white men knew Indians, a few days before that, Marten performed the shaking tent. If they had asked for his help, they could have found out exactly what happened.

* * *

Jean Lindokken: Postmaster Bill Hendry was at times a hard man to deal with at his post. The Caribou Lake post had many debts and Hendry didn't want anybody pulling anything over his eyes. One man alienated was Alfred Meekis, son of Big Trap.

Anyway, in the fall of the year 1933, Hendry sent his clerk Alfred Sterling, along with Moses Meekis, a son of Alfred Meekis, down to Windy Lake to haul up whitefish. They had a dog team with them to return after freeze-up. For some reason, Moses Meekis quit the job and left Sterling there alone. So, William Hendry closed the store and went down to get his clerk.

Oscar Lindokken came by the Caribou Lake to get a letter for me but the post was locked and Oscar noticed foot tracks and marks where a canoe had been pulled through the snow and shoved out into the water of Caribou Lake. Oscar never

Chief Robert Fiddler on his death bed, 1940.
Collection, Thomas Fiddler.

thought anything of it and returned two days later to discover no one had returned to the post.

Then Oscar met some of the people and they made it known that the storekeepers were not just away – they were missing.

Oscar sent word to the outpost manager at Sandy Lake to come to Caribou Lake. Then Oscar and some of the men went down to investigate.

The HBC men were not to be seen. Tea was left frozen in their cups in their tent. Their clothes were all in the tent. All the sled dogs were gone except the lead dog, 'Spinach.'

The lead dog, for some reason, hated the sight of Alfred Meekis.

There were signs of gunshots in the area but the Meekis' said they had been hunting around there.

The only sign of these men that was found the following spring was a canoe paddle floating in the river.

* * *

The winter following William Hendry's and Alfred Sterling's disappearance is a hard one for Robert Fiddler and the Sucker people. K.C. Roseborough, the replacement for Hendry at Caribou Lake, writes in his journal at the HBC post.

December 5th: 'Snowing a very bad day for flying, no hope of plane today. More of the Meekis bunch in today. All want to stay here & eat.

December 6th: 'Snowing & still very little hope of plane. Chief Fiddler tribe in from Sandy hungry as usual, these people are the best panhandlers in the world.'

December 7th: 'North wind, cold and cloudy, still no plane, a lot of Indians here & all hungry, still begging for rations.'[46]

When the winter snows turn into the spring melt and the river unlocks from ice there is 'No sign of the remains of Hendry & Sterling, except for a paddle which they had apparently used for sounding ice.' William Hendry and Alfred Sterling are

Island Lake HBC Post, 1909. Photo, P.H. Godsell.
Courtesy, Glenbow Alberta Institute, Calgary.

gone off forever. Their disappearance will remain an unsolved mystery in the forests.

Two years after the disappearance of the two HBC men another death through the ice occurs. It happens to the only Sucker clansman that remains at Caribou Lake, Thompson Quill, the crawler, and son of the late Joseph Fiddler. Thompson is an uncle of Thomas, in relationship, he was more of a father to Thomas, when Thomas was a youth at Caribou and Windy Lakes. Great respect, even awe, is awarded Thompson Quill because of the combination of talents Thompson has along with his serious physical limitations. It was inspiring for other men to see a clansman who could not walk, survive in the forest where a man needed all his faculties in gaining a living. For Thompson, in the tradition of Sucker clansmen, played the fiddle; operated the shaking tent; trapped and hunted; and travelled extensively on the lakes. Only the odds for long survival were always loaded against Thompson Quill. He lived for almost sixty years before news reached Big Sandy Lake in the fall of 1936 that 'the crawler' had passed beyond. He had fallen through the ice on Caribou Lake and drowned.

Over a quarter of a century had passed at the time of Thompson Quill's death, since Treaty Commissioner John Semmens had canoed down Caribou Lake to meet with Robert Fiddler and the Sucker, Pelican and Crane clans in 1910. No reserve grounds had been officially granted to the clansmen. In 1929, Commissioner Awrey, had promised Robert Fiddler that a reserve would be granted along the river between Narrows Lake and Big Sandy Lake. It was known from prospecting activity that gold bearing ore existed in these grounds selected by Robert Fiddler. The Province of Ontario, with its greed for wealth, was reluctant to legitimize the grounds that had been selected as a reserve. Robert Fiddler, faced with Ontario's avarice, would not live long enough to see the meagre seventeen square miles along the river made an official reserve.

PART FIVE

ADAM FIDDLER

ADAM FIDDLER

He was divinely appointed to be a priest unto his people

WHEN HE WAS A YOUNG MAN Adam Fiddler, younger brother of the Sucker clan leader, Robert Fiddler, was known to have had 'a remarkable spiritual experience.' A figure of Jesus Christ, the white leader in after-life came to Adam in a dream. This revelation occurred sometime after Adam's 1901 journey to Norway House with the Methodist missionary, Frederick Stevens. Jesus Christ, an other-than-human, became a guide, for Adam Fiddler was able to learn much of Christianity through the syllabic bibles that had been printed and from his conversations with Stevens. Literate in syllabics, as were most members, Adam kept records of his spiritual activities in a set of books.

Adam, however, was cautious in what he accepted from Christian spiritualism for he was not a foolish man. He did not discard what he found good and necessary in his forest beliefs and he is best described as a Holy Man among the clansmen rather than a Methodist Christian. Adam Fiddler was a Sucker clansman who could confront windigo, utilize the shaking tent, issue prophecies, and sing over his drum. Adam Fiddler was more than a Christian.

Adam's adoption of some Christian beliefs, though, did start a process of change away from some of the ancient ways.

* * *

Thomas Fiddler: When Adam Fiddler was married, he dreamt a vision – a certain light came and after he knew he was going to receive the Lord Jesus. After this things started to change. Religion caused people to reject supernatural powers.

But they believed, before, when a baby died in a tikanogan,

the spirit of the baby was still in that tikanogan. People believed that through the shaking tent a person could relive, even babies could relive. Through the shaking tent, they asked the dead baby – now in the beyond and the grave – to do favours for the people.

People kept certain things that belonged to a dead person. For dead men they keep items that were used in living – an axe, gun, or trap. For dead women they keep the clothes that the deceased wore. For babies they keep clothing. People that believe in the shaking tent would take these belongings and communicate with the dead person. They would ask the dead person to help them cure illness. People had majestic powers to do this.

In Adam's dream, it was shown that people shouldn't falsely use the shaking tent between the living and the dead. Adam believed the personal things of the dead should be put away and not used. Adam believed it was better to burn the belongings of the dead people; leave them dead and not communicate with them anymore.

This all happened to Adam, just after he was married; his first wife had a child and the child died. It was around this time he changed.

My mother used to tell me that there were deep feelings between herself and Adam. They shared a brother-sister love. When Adam lost his son he was in despair and my mother had a son. This son represented the son that Adam lost.

Adam was actually in a trance or a coma after the loss of his son. He didn't come out of this state until my mother had her son. Adam told my mother when her child was born: 'Put the baby behind my back and let him breathe in my ear before I turn around to look at him.'

I was this son who was put to his ear.

At this time of Adam's vision, people started to question conjuring. A controversy occurred between Adam and the rest of the Sandy Lakers, for Adam was introducing Christianity. It was Adam who turned everyone toward Christianity.

'No more,' Adam told the people, 'if you don't believe in conjuring it won't happen. What you do not believe in, will not happen.'

Adam still used the shaking tent after this but it was for good. He used the shaking tent to get rid of bad things. Adam said: 'As the wind blows and the tent shakes, it washes our sins away.'

Adam still beat his drums as an expression of joy to Manitou. When Adam used these powers, he didn't do it secretly.

It was a minister* from Island Lake that persuaded Adam that he should become a minister for the Methodists.

* * *

Adam Fiddler's spiritual services for the Sucker and Pelican clans were not supervised by Christian missionaries in the first decade of the twentieth century. As a Holy Man, his teachings were individualistic and only tenuously connected to the Toronto based Methodists through their missionaries at Island Lake. Then, in the summer of 1913, Frederick Stevens canoed down Caribou Lake to meet with Robert and Adam Fiddler for the first time in twelve years. Robert, the leader, was not impressed that the missionaries' arrival had any import whatsoever. Western craziness delivered by a missionary's sermons told the clansmen how they should see the forests, how to live their lives, how to mate, and how to think away from custom.

'My experience in life has taught me that all men are liars,' Robert Fiddler, the leader, faces Stevens, 'especially missionaries. You may never come back; we see you now but we may never see you again.'

Adam Fiddler is less adamant toward Stevens than clan leader Robert. A brotherly bond had existed between Stevens and Adam Fiddler, since the starvation times of 1899-1900, and this relationship would grow to a source of embarrassment in the United Church in later years. In 1913, however, Adam Fiddler told Stevens the nature of his spiritual teachings: 'I cannot baptize children but I pray with the parents and urge them to live for Manitou. When a couple comes together, I pray to Manitou, that He will bless their union.'

After Stevens leaves Caribou Lake, a story is spread among

*Reverend Frederick George Stevens

Adam Fiddler's Methodist Church, Caribou Lake, 1917.
Courtesy, United Church Archives, Toronto.

the clans. Adam Fiddler is going to build a log church in the forests roamed by Weesakayjac. Many clansmen must have had doubts that this event would occur for up until this time the only people who built log structures in the forest were the HBC. Adam Fiddler's log church will have its hardware shipped to HBC Berens River on Lake Winnipeg, by Winnipeg Methodists and Frederick Stevens.

By summer 1915, Robert Fiddler has placed a value on some important Christian ritual but he has given up on distant missionaries for leadership. Robert, the leader, presses his brother, Adam, and delivers confidence that he, Adam, should administer the communion sacraments of Christianity. After this request from Robert, Adam consents to give the sacraments to the Sucker and Pelican clans.

Work proceeds on Adam's church on the Treaty point at Caribou Lake. In 1917 the church is completed – 'a very fine church.' Adam has, with the people, built a smaller church than he had intended but it is 28 by 18 feet and erected with care. The door frame is hand carved, the floor whipsawed and planed. It has a bell tower. It appears in Caribou Lake as a solid structure.

This same summer, Adam Fiddler decides he will journey with his nephew, Moses, to the city of Winnipeg to attend a Methodist Conference. It is his first visit to the edge of the grassy lands where there is now a city of 150,000 western people. It is a journey by canoe down the Berens River valley, then by steam boat across Lake Winnipeg, by electric trolley from Selkirk into the city. The streets are filled with soldiers, a great war is on among the western people in Europe. The Conference sessions are all in English, and Adam and Moses cannot speak a word. The only participation they have in the Conference is singing along in Cree with some of the common hymns in their syllabic books. Adam is so shocked by all this – it is difficult to believe what he sees – he turns ill. The next morning he and Moses are back on the steamer out of Selkirk as it plows through the muddy Winnipeg for Berens River. Adam says on his return, it is almost impossible to believe the size of the white man's churches.

Mrs. Robert Fiddler, 1946. Photo Lloyd Bartlett.

In the eyes of Methodist missionary Frederick G. Stevens, Adam Fiddler's stature grows. There is admiration for Adam Fiddler's strength as a Holy Man among the Sucker people. 'Truly he was divinely appointed to be a priest unto his people,' Stevens writes.

In 1918, 'Adam Fiddler had had a hard winter, as he had sickness in his family, his adopted son having died after a long illness.'

It is also in this same time that a teacher comes to Caribou Lake to make the children wise in western ways. The Crane hunters – from Cliff Dweller Lake who come to Caribou Lake for Treaty, take their children out of school. The reason they state: 'We do not want our children's names taken away. The teacher tells our children not to kill little birds. We do not want our children taught that.' The Cranes protest the strange ways of western teachings.

The incursion of westernized teachers into the forests of the clansmen around Caribou Lake is brief, limited to the summers of 1918 and 1919. Clansmen live throughout the forest and have not settled in a permanent site.

The Sucker, Pelican and Crane clans were still living the nomadic life and Adam Fiddler had to travel from camp to camp to talk to the folk about the Jesus spirit. The church at Caribou Lake was busy in the summers but in the winters Adam moved about to keep contact with the people. Edward Rae tells about the Holy Man's activities.

* * *

Edward Rae: My father, John Rae, passed away and I went to live with Adam Fiddler. I was less than ten years old at this time. Adam's camp was on the east end of Caribou Lake. In the winter time Adam's camp was southeast of Caribou Lake, down at Two Beach Lake, Apps Lake, or over at Owl Lake.

Adam travelled all over this territory in the winter time and he had only a dog team. Of course, he was working for nothing. He would go to a camp for a night, hold a service, then go back home, and then make another trip from there. All he

Giff Swartman (Indian Agent), Chief Thomas Fiddler,
Reverend Frederick G. Stevens. Photo, Lloyd Bartlett.

carried on these trips was food for himself and his dogs. If the people had extra moose meat or rabbits, they usually gave it to Adam to take home. He was appreciated by the people.

Adam's service didn't have to be on Sunday. It was a question of when he arrived. Then he held services.

During the real coldness and at break-up he didn't travel.

He had to trap, too. He had his trap line when he was travelling around in those days. Adam was a real good trapper and he had lots of success. Sometimes Adam would get over $1,000 worth of fur by Christmas time.

Practically everybody went to the church that Adam built. They sang gospel songs and read the Bible at church services. Adam preached and later on Moses Fiddler helped him. The only thing they had in that church was an organ. Mooniyas and Alfred Fiddler used to play it.

In the days when Adam Fiddler was a preacher, he told us missionaries would be coming all over the north in the future. Adam said these missionaries would have everything they needed, lots of resources, even airplanes. He even said what these missionaries would preach about. Adam said: 'These missionaries will show everything that they have while they preach to you.'

Adam said all this right in church so everybody would hear.

Adam said: 'There will be other preachers. Just watch for them. They will have everything, food, money, clothes, everything. Just watch for him and keep your own church.'

* * *

I saw Adam Fiddler use the shaking tent a lot. Adam never tried to use it for evil. He was a medicine man. When he used the drum, it is only for the good of the people. When he did his tent shaking, he found out the kind of a disease a person has. One person he healed was Mary Meekis of Sandy Lake. She had a disease and Adam healed her through tent shaking. The side of her thumb was sore and infected. It started swelling and she almost died from that disease in her thumb. But Adam found out what was wrong with her through the shaking tent — what kind of disease she had — and he healed her.

The disease she had – some of the old men said that Mary's husband had dreamed of a large penis. Mary tried to put her thumb over the end of this penis, where the little hole was. It was after this dream that Mary got the disease in her thumb. But, she was healed by Adam through tent shaking. Adam also used roots of trees; he boiled these things and had Mary soak her thumb in this medicine. He also wrapped a cloth around it to keep it wet for a long period. Ever since they figured out where the disease came from, it remained healed.

They smoke for healing people too. After the shaking tent, they come out with tobacco. That tobacco is round like a marble but when they got it ready, it amounted to two pipe loads. I have seen them obtain that tobacco by putting a white cloth on a table and that tobacco would appear under it. I saw Adam Fiddler do this when he had nothing to smoke.

Another incredible thing that Adam used to do – this was told to me – if Adam wanted to heal somebody he would walk up to a cliff and walk in to get some medicine. He would see the dwellers in the cliffs. Adam got quite a bit of his medicine in there. With this medicine he would heal a person when he was really sick. People paid for the medicine by giving something that was valuable, like a gun or an axe, to Adam.

Adam was a taller man than Robert Fiddler. They were both pretty big. There is a strong resemblance between Adam Fiddler and Thomas Fiddler both in the body and in the face.

* * *

One time I was out trapping with Monias Fiddler, Adam Fiddler's son, and I nearly lost myself. It was early spring. The snow was melting. I went out moose hunting all day and finally saw tracks that went into a small lake. I followed the tracks and the moose came toward me. I shot it and started to butcher it up.

It was just before dusk and it started snowing and blowing so I decided to go. By the time I got to the other end of that lake my moccasins and socks were soaken wet. I didn't know which way to go. I kept walking until I came to another small lake. It was foggy and I saw what looked like a light in the mist. Still, I didn't know which way to go.

I knew I was lost. My moccasins were frozen and I was getting cold. I figured it was the end; I was going to die. After I reached the end of the little lake, I put a marker on the ice and went up on the land to the place where I would die. On the land, I packed down the snow and lay there with my arms folded over my chest. I put my cap over my eyes. While I was laying there I fell asleep.

I thought I heard someone saying, 'Get up and go home!' I woke up and heard a second voice saying this. The third time I heard a voice saying the same thing. I struggled to my feet and I saw a trail blazed with a blue light through the trees and I could see a path. I had the moose's heart in my sack and I knew I wouldn't get lost on that path.

I was a person who thought he owned his own life but I also thought something else was watching over me.

Then I started walking home. I couldn't feel my feet, only my ankles. The rest of my feet were frozen solid. I got home to our camp and went inside. I said to Monias; 'I have destroyed myself but something brought me home.'

Monias asked me; 'What happened, did you shoot yourself?'

I sat down and he cut my moccasins and socks off my feet. My feet were frozen like rocks. Monias took one look at my feet and started to cry.

Then he told me: 'You had better eat before you start to feel the pain from your feet.'

Monias went out and got our toboggan and he made a frame to put me on. He put me in a couple of sleeping bags and we started back to the main camp. When we left it was just starting to be dawn. It took us all day to get back to the main camp, Adam Fiddler's camp on Two Beach Lake.

At first, Adam just soaked my feet in water. I don't know what he put in the water. It was so painful I couldn't fall asleep for four nights. Adam kept soaking my feet until the skin started to peel. On one of those nights, I dreamt someone came through the door. It looked like a man all dressed in metal.

This man grabbed me and put me on my feet. After this, the pain was gone and I began to sleep real well.

Then Adam got the second layer of bark off the balsam tree and he boiled that. He took it out of the pot, beat it to a pulp and put that on my feet. Everyday, he washed my feet and changed the pulp on my feet. Later he covered my feet with some kind of material and rabbit skin slippers.

At this time I didn't bother much with thinking about Manitou, but he showed me that time. I couldn't even read syllabics before this happened. While I was recovering, syllabics came to me and I could read syllabics after this.

I was in bed for about a month, then I had to use sticks for crutches. When I got up, I was dizzy from looking down at the ground from so high up.

* * *

In the meantime, western influence on the clansmen was to gain momentum. In 1936 a Roman Catholic Mission was built on the chosen grounds of the clansmen. From the turn of the century, Christian religion, modified through the teachings of Sucker Holy Man, Adam Fiddler, had been the sole Christian input in the lives of the clansmen.

After the clansmen had migrated to Big Sandy Lake in 1926-28, Adam built another log church along the river to preach the benefits of Jesus Christ as a guiding being. In this role, he had periodic support from Reverend Frederick Stevens, the Methodist Missionary, who was now a minister of the United Church of Canada. Occasionally, Stevens saw to it that clothes and hardware were shipped up through Berens River to Adam Fiddler for dispersal to the people. But, in 1936 a large Roman Catholic mission was built on the chosen reserve grounds at Sandy Lake. By this time, Adam Fiddler had been a practising Holy Man for over three decades and he was now seventy-one years old. Adam's prophecies that more and wealthy missionaries would come to the boreal forest had come true. He did not predict, however, that it would be his younger brother, Jean Batiste Fiddler, who would invite the Roman Catholic missionaries to come to Sandy Lake.

Thomas Fiddler: At Caribou Lake, there were no Catholics over there or priests of any sort. Did you ever hear when the first priests came down to Sandy Lake area? I do not actually know what year a priest came in but I remember we had lived for quite awhile in Sandy Lake before the priest came.

During this time, Jean Batiste Fiddler, went down to Island Lake to visit. When he returned he did not tell people that he invited the priest to come over. It was about March 20th and the snow had melted off the lakes, leaving only ice.

It was during the time Adam Fiddler came for a visit from over by Setting Net Lake. Adam Fiddler was living at my house. All of a sudden a plane landed near my house.

Well, Jean Batiste hadn't told any of us the priest was coming over.

Robert Fiddler was still walking around, good and strong, and we went down to where the plane landed.

My father, Robert, asked Jean Batiste: 'Are you a Catholic?'

Well he didn't understand what he had said, but Jean Batiste replied: 'Yes, but temporarily, I'm not a minister.'

At the same time the plane flew in, two dog teams came over with a priest. The priest had a fish net with him and it was the first time we saw a 'jigger' used to set nets beneath the ice in the winter.

In the summer Father Dubeau and Brother Dussalt began to make lumber for the mission house. At the same time Father Dubeau made a garden, not just a small garden but a large one. At the same time he fished; sort of commercial fished. I guess he was a priest, father, farmer and fisherman at the same time. He also looked after medical supplies and worked as a nurse. He helped a lot of people in those days.

My old house is down by the river – the priest gave me lumber to use to build that house. I pulled in logs for his lumber mill and that's why I got the lumber. At this time I had one of those big old fashioned Johnson motors – a great big thing. I pulled down about one hundred and twenty-five logs to the saw mill. The priest gave me the gas to pull the logs with my motor. The told me: 'For every log you bring in, you will get half the lumber and I will get the other half.'

Angus Rae and Family, 1946. Photo, Lloyd Bartlett.

I took the lumber from the sawmill down to the river and, built that house.

Old Adam Fiddler's response to the extensive Roman Catholic mission was to build a larger church for his followers. He sent a letter to Reverend J.A. Cormie in 1939, requesting assistance in this endeavour; Cormie replies, 'I wish you would explain to Adam Fiddler that we appreciate all he had done but that the Board of Home Missions does not think it is advisable at the present time at least, to make the large expenditures on buildings that would be necessary in an isolated post such as that.'

In the summer of 1940, Reverend Frederick Stevens flew into the Berens River Mine and then journeyed by boat to Sandy Lake to visit with Fiddler. As far as Stevens was concerned, 'the people there have organized their religious life in a very satisfactory way among themselves.' Following Stevens' visit with Adam, the Norway House Presbytery recommended that $500 be granted for a new church at Sandy Lake. The Presbytery also pointed out that Adam's congregation had endured 'throughout many long years, in the face of much discouragement, and lack of support and encouragement from the church of their choice, the United Church of Canada.'

In the summer of 1940, Robert Fiddler, the leader of the people died and his eldest surviving son, Thomas Fiddler, became Chief. Through this grieving time old Adam Fiddler kept his health and spirit strong and proceeded to order supplies for the new church. For, Adam knew that if the Board of Home Missions would not pay for the materials, Frederick Stevens would raise the funds by soliciting the required cash from the various United Church congregations in Winnipeg.

The reaction of the Secretary of the Board of Home Missions, Reverend Robert Cochrane, in Toronto, toward Stevens' involvement at Sandy Lake and knowledge that he would solicit funds was one of frustration. But in the winter of 1941, lumber, shingles, doors, windows, for Adam's church, were on a tractor train winding its way north to the Berens River Mine, where this material, purchased by Stevens with funds from Winnipeg Churches, would be picked up by the Sandy Lakers.

The United Church built by Adam Fiddler, along the river between Sandy Lake and Narrows Lake, is thirty by forty-one feet and is white shingled. The walls are log hewn. Its doorway faces the east where the daylight rises and it has eight windows representing the spiritual number of the parts of a wabino thanksgiving feast. (A new version of this church built in the late 60s would be called 'The Adam Fiddler United Church.')

PART SIX

CHIEF THOMAS FIDDLER

CHIEF THOMAS FIDDLER

*It seemed to be generally agreed ... that the Chief from
Sandy Lake Band was the most powerful magician in the
area.*

WHEN ROBERT FIDDLER DIED in 1940, tradition held. His eldest surviving son, Thomas Fiddler, becomes leader of the
Sucker people at Sandy Lake. This ancient tradition reaches
back into the mists in the forest. Now, however, an elected
office of 'Chief' imposed by the Department of Indian Affairs,
is included with Thomas Fiddler's hereditary status.

* * *

Thomas Fiddler: You can easily understand how they do it in
England. When my father, Robert, died I automatically took
over as chief. My oldest brother, Henry, was living away over
at Island Lake and he was already chief of the people there.
Isaac and Moses, my other brothers, were gone. Alfred,
another brother, was younger.

Lots of people said Francis Meekis, my father's counsellor,
should be chief. But the important men said they shouldn't do
this. These men said that since Robert Fiddler was chief for
more than thirty years, they should think of me as Robert Fiddler.

When I became chief I stayed working at the mine (Berens
River Mine). I had to make a living for my family and we
would have starved if I sat around Sandy Lake.

So Francis Meekis became my counsellor. Francis wasn't a
man who was easily discouraged. He always looked for the
best in people. He was a good person himself. It was Francis
Meekis who had to eat his rabbit skin jacket back when the
people were starving. He used to say that he didn't remember
his father. When he was a little boy he was taken care of by his

uncle, Joseph Meekis. It was when he was a little boy he had to eat this rabbit skin jacket. I often heard him talk of how he had to eat little pieces of meat off bones.

In relationship he was my brother-in-law. His sister was my wife. Actually, my wife was a first cousin. Francis' real father was named David Meekis.*

I often heard Francis say the only reason he was alive was he ate his rabbit skin jacket and scraps off bones. I used to kid him that was the reason he was so small. He didn't eat properly. When his uncle died I can faintly remember. Then Adam Fiddler took care of him. Adam taught him how to hunt and trap. I could safely say Francis Meekis was the best worker, trapper, hunter in Sandy Lake during his manhood.

At this time Francis used to kill lots of moose and caught many furs. Francis used to say, 'Just imagine, I used to eat bones, now I have so much.' When we hauled freight, Francis always worked with us. He always worked with us even when trapping. When we were at Caribou Lake, that's when he first became a counsellor to Robert Fiddler.

*Francis' father, David Meekis of the Pelican clan, died as a result of windigo possession in 1898.

* * *

Francis Meekis of the Pelican people was from another forest clan who have long been allies and who are closely interrelated by marriages to the Suckers. This alliance was bonded again when the elder, Francis, stayed on as Thomas' counsellor after he had held the position for fifteen years with Robert Fiddler.

During the operation of the Berens River Mine, Chief Thomas Fiddler works there to support his family. Many of the clansmen do this for the price of fur makes it difficult to live off the land. As Chief of the Deer Lake Band, Thomas faced several problems, foremost of which was the question of reserve land. Thirty-four years after a treaty and fifteen years after Commissioners Cain and Awrey visited Sandy Lake, no reserve grounds have been granted there.

Four days after Christmas in 1944, Thomas writes a syllabic letter to Reverend Frederick Stevens explaining:

> Now, one big thing I want to tell you.... This is about our reserve. Just now we are being attacked by the Roman Catholics. They are trying to take away part of our reserve.... It can't be right for anyone to want to steal. Who is responsible to look after this?
>
> I want to tell you something about these RCs. This winter they surveyed a line inside our reserve. You know this is theft or looks like it. The priest ... teaches the ten commandments and then does the things the commandments tell us not to do. How is that for the work of the priest at Sandy Lake?
>
> I tell you no Indian was asked about this land. I would like this to be taken up by the law.[47]

But the law that all clansmen have to deal with is western law and this legal system as used in the boreal forest, is utilized to oppress and usurp the rights of the clans. The death of clan leader, Jack Fiddler; the appeal process of Joseph Fiddler; the arrest of Jimmy Kakagamick; and the non-negotiation of treaties, provide ample evidence of the thrust of western intent. So, the reply to Thomas Fiddler's complaints are concise, the St. Bernadette Mission can take title to land between Big Sandy Lake and Narrows Lake because, 'there is legally no Reserve. The reason for the delay is that three mining claims have been located on what would be reserve land.' To their credit, the St. Bernadette Mission withdraws their claims and, in 1947, the Government of Ontario, now assured that clansmen are not getting land of much value, agree to give title to the reserve at Sandy Lake.

Treaty payments of five dollars per clansman still takes place at the reserve grounds in the boreal forest every summer. The Department of Indian Affairs agent from Sioux Lookout makes a visit through the forest every summer to Osnaburgh, Pikangikum, Caribou Lake, Sandy Lake, Fishtrap Lake, Big Trout Lake, Round Lake, Fort Severn, Lansdowne House, Winisk and Lac Seul to pay all the people.

The summer of 1949 is different, however; a red coated soldier of the R.C.M.P. is with the treaty party. This soldier, Constable J.G. Russell is an agent. Russell writes a report about Thomas Fiddler. Russell's report says.

On three occasions in the past year, THOMAS FIDDLER, Chief of the Sandy Lake Band ... had visited ... Caribou Lake ... for the purpose of collecting money to enable him to go to Winnipeg. The purpose of the visit ... is to organize an Indian Federation through a group of lawyers residing somewhere on James Ave. in Winnipeg, Man.

This THOMAS FIDDLER has been causing agitation among the Indians for some time by stating that the original Treaty has not been fulfilled and that the Indians should do something about it.

... at Caribou Lake and at the General Meeting which most of the 100 Indians residing there, attended, Supt. Swartman mentioned the collection of money for another Government. He stated that there was only one Government and one Flag, with one King for all of us.

... the Counsellor of the Band ... made no reply whatsoever to Supt. Swartman's remarks on the collection of Money.

At Sandy Lake ... the Indian Agent mentioned a report of the Kenora Detachment with regard to breaking in of the Mine in the vicinity of Sandy Lake. According to Mr. Swartman's remarks definite proof had been established to the fact that Indians had been involved. In his reply THOMAS FIDDLER the Chief stated that before the Indian Agent made any rash statements he had better have proof of his remarks as Indians were always being blamed for troubles in the Area.

It must be noted at this time that in questioning the Post Managers of the Hudson's Bay Company and Indians throughout the Northern part of the Province of Ontario, that all were unanimous in their condemnation of the Sandy Lake Band and their Chief, THOMAS FIDDLER as surly and uncooperative. This fact was substantiated by Mr. Cam Currie and Mr. Gordon Miles of the

Ontario Lands and Forests Dept., both of whom have had long experience in the North Country. In their estimation this is directly due to the attitude taken and the advice given by their Chief.[48]

The Royal Canadian Mounted Police, much respected by westerners in Canada, continued to prove by Russell's report on Thomas Fiddler, that their behaviour in regard to boreal clansmen has been political in action.

Thomas Fiddler just laughs at being called an agitator, unsurly and uncooperative, and shows a Government of Ontario citation congratulating him on his being an exemplary citizen of the Province. 'I have always spoken out for my people,' he says.

In 1948-49, the Berens River Mine had closed when the price of zinc fell and many of the clansmen migrated south to work in the gold mines in the Red Lake District. Thomas Fiddler takes his family down to Red Lake for awhile. While he is there his son, Abel, tells us.

* * *

Abel Fiddler: You know when you first asked me about the Suckers, I didn't know what you were talking about. Later I remembered that in the fifties when dad went out to Red Lake to live for awhile that the people around there called him the 'Sucker Chief.' There were many that used to visit him and they brought him bags of groceries or a shirt. Many of the men that worked in the mine were called by the other Indians – the Sucker men. When I remembered this from that time, I know what you were talking about.

* * *

But, Red Lake is one hundred and forty air miles south of Big Sandy Lake and Thomas decided that he could hardly be an effective leader that far away from most of his people. So, he and his family return to the shores of the Bay River. His skills as a traditional leader are needed.

Thomas Fiddler: When I was over forty winters old I began to use the drum. From the time I started this, until two years later, that was when I really knew about the drum. While I was using drums, I made medicines for at least two years. The people had asked me if I could make medicines. After two years of healing the sick, I could feel something in my hands.

When a child has cramps, when I touched and rubbed all over, the child usually responds. During this time, Meekis' son – he was just a young baby – it was toward the Christmas time – had cramps all over his body. Before I saw the child an old lady said they kept this baby alive by breathing into its mouth.

When this happened they asked me to come to Meekis' lodge. I went in the lodge, took off my coat, rolled up my sleeves, then stood by the fire so my hands would be warm.

When I touched the baby I knew and I said to the people: 'I can heal the child with my hands.'

I really believed that I could, and at this time the baby could not breathe without the help of the old woman.

After I finished rubbing this child all over, he was well again.

For medicines, I dreamt that I went over to the big hill at Windy Lake. I believe this to be the same place my grandfather went for his medicine.

In this dream, I went up to the hill and went right inside it. Inside the hill I saw cave dwellers grouped together. There was one leader inside the hill but I couldn't see him. But the lower leaders told me I was to stay three nights with the leader. I stayed for three nights and didn't see the leader at all. But the purpose of this dream was to let me know how to get medicine from there to help the people.

Then, when people have different sicknesses, I just know what to get to make medicine.

**

By 1950, Thomas Fiddler and the clan people of the boreal forest have experienced the introduction of many changes in the boreal forest. The imposition of treaty in 1910 has supplied the yearly benefit of survival rations, and money to deal away at the HBC store. Airplanes fly the skies above the forest. Outboard motors drive manufactured canoes up and down the lakes and rivers of the Bay River. A mining town and all its technology has arisen in the heart of Sucker clan lands, and then faded away after a decade. The boon of western medicine has been introduced in the lands of Weesakayjac and a migration of some clansmen to the south to work in other mines has occurred. There has been much adoption of western technology and practise among the native clansmen.

During the fifties changes continue in the village at Sandy Lake. Effective medicine, baby bonuses, and the clansmen's great regard for children result in a rapidly growing population. In 1955, the Northern Light Gospel Mission (Mennonites) establish themselves in several places in the forest, including Caribou and Sandy Lake. This results in another wedge in the loyalties of the people on the reserve. In the fall of 1956, a nursing station with two attending R.N.s is completed at Big Sandy. Three years later, Holyman Adam Fiddler passed away at ninety-four. A year round elementary school is opened at Sandy Lake in 1961 and this removes the necessity of sending children away to residential schools. It is Thomas Fiddler who oversees these changes for his people. But in 1968, his beloved wife, Mary Ann, passes away and this is the cause of a deep and profound grief for the clan leader. The strain causes Thomas to resign his elected position as Chief of the 'Deer Lake Band.' Then his own health deteriorates and Thomas goes out to the Fort William Sanitorium because he has active tuberculosis. His stay there is not long; he recovers quickly and returns to the north.

During Thomas Fiddler's 28 years as the elected Chief not a single person is taken away by the police nor is there a single alcohol-related death among the clan folk. This is an achievement that most other municipal leaders in Canada would be hard pressed to match.

Retirement does not come to Thomas Fiddler, though he gives up his elected position as leader or 'Chief.' He becomes

Adam Fiddler's gravestone; Adam's son Monias Fiddler
seated; Ahab Rae, standing. Photo, Yvonne Nipe.

active with Grand Council Treaty Number Nine. This native organization represents all the native reserves across northern Ontario. Later, in 1977, the organization declares nation status and is called the Nishnawbe-Aski Nation. Thomas Fiddler joins the Circle of Elders in Nishnawbe-Aski which attempts to deal with all the plans being made for the boreal forest north of Lake Superior. In 1976, the Province of Ontario gives a huge tract of land to a paper company, Reed International, the company responsible for polluting the Wabigoon and Winnipeg Rivers with mercury from its plant at Dryden, Ontario. A natural gas pipeline from the high arctic is planned to come across the clan folks land on its way to southern markets. There are vague plans for river diversions on the Albany River. In response to native peoples' outcries a *Royal Commission On The Northern Environment* is ordered by the Province of Ontario. These intrusions lead an elder from Big Trout Lake to lament:

* * *

Jeremiah Sainnawap: I always go along when the chiefs have meetings in the big cities. They often discuss our land. They are afraid that our land will someday be destroyed.

The water is being polluted and the fish are being poisoned. Everything that grows is being threatened. We fear that there may be nothing left for our future generations to hunt and trap and live off the land.

I believe the white people will take over our land. There are too many white people here now and too many of their works. The ways they travel are fast, just like the wind.

The chiefs believe that the Indian people own the land. They were born on this land and so were their greatgrand-fathers. The people will continue to be worried about the land.

The white man wants everything. It is hard to say yes to him when what he wants is something that is precious to us.

James Linklater (The Marten), 1971.
Photo, James Stevens.

There is one thing we know. God made everything we see in the world – everything that grows – all living things. Only God can say, 'This is my land.' He loves every being that lives on his land.

* * *

Thomas Fiddler has his deep concerns also, especially about pulp and paper companies. When a lawyer for the *Royal Commission On The Northern Environment* asks Thomas Fiddler how he would view the cutting of trees if they can be regrown and jobs would be given to his people, he replied: 'I have never seen anyone grow a forest. Now, I have a question for you. There is a lot of land in Canada that does not have trees. Why don't these companies plant trees and grow their forests there?'

This concern for his people and the land keeps Thomas Fiddler active, even in his eighties. In 1984, the Province of Ontario awards him with a Bicentennial Metal. At the convocation for this award, he is given the honorary title, Chief Emeritus, The Sucker leader stands proudly in wearing it.

* * *

Thomas Fiddler: I think about a question that was asked of me. It was: What do I think of myself being an Anishinaapi – an Indian? Do I like being Indian? Do I enjoy living?

I said, I believe Manitou made this light. I believe that Manitou made every Creature who lives on this earth. I also believe that Manitou made plants, and every vegetation that is growing on this earth; there are so many things with various and different shapes. There are so many things both above in the air and below in the water – and Manitou made these things. I really believe that Manitou thought about it when He began creating this world. To this we give greatest respect.

I said I like my life because Manitou willed it that I be on this earth. Manitou willed it that I should be here and Manitou wants me to keep my life existing. If I destroyed my life early, I don't think Manitou would like this. If I keep my life long I think Manitou would like this. I believe that every human being should hold his life valuable and should value this earth. I believe this is what Manitou wants of us.

I said, I am happy that I am an Indian.

I said Manitou didn't make a mistake by not giving me a tongue to speak English. Manitou didn't make a mistake when He put the white men across the ocean.

And Manitou didn't make a mistake when he made me an Indian.

* * *

APPENDIX ONE: CLAN GEOGRAPHY

Rivers – Clan Names	*Western Names*
The Thunderbird River	Hayes River
The Bay River	Severn River
Gooseshit River	Flanagan River
The Groundhog River	Winisk River
The Blocked River	Attawapiskat River
The Rushing or Big River	Albany River
The Moose River	Moose River

Lakes – Clan Names	*Western Names*
Bearberry Lake	Warwick Lake
Big Lake	McDowell Lake
Caribou Lake	Deer Lake
Cliff Dweller Lake	North Spirit Lake
Fishweir Lake	Bearskin Lake
Island Lake	Island Lake
Narrows Lake	Finger Lake
Owl Lake	McGuinness Lake
Red Lake	Red Lake
Big Sandy Lake	Sandy Lake
Swampy Lake	Lake St. Joseph
Two Beach Lake	Kennedy Lake
White Pine Narrows Lake	Lac Seul
Windy Lake	Favourable Lake

APPENDIX TWO: INDEX TO ORAL STORIES

APPENDIX THREE: BIOGRAPHIES

Chief Jacob Berens (Light Passing Across The Sky): Jacob Berens was born in 1830, the year of Halley's Comet. He became the first elected Chief of Berens River and Little Grand Rapids and was signatory to Treaty Number Five signed at Berens River in September, 1875. As a young man he was a brigade captain on the yorkboats out of York Factory, and Norway House. He married, Mary MacKay, the daughter of William MacKay, an HBC postmaster. Berens died at Berens River in July 1916.

William 'Big Bill' Campbell: Born 1866. William Campbell was the son of George McDonald Campbell and Annie Brander and was raised in the village of Kyleakin, Isle of Skye, Scotland. He joined the Hudson's Bay Company as an apprentice clerk in 1885. He had postings at York Factory, Oxford House, God's Lake, Red Sucker Lake, Island Lake and Norway House. Campbell wrote a detailed description of his experience with the Hudson's Bay Company that covered the years 1885-1910. (The Narrative of 'Big Bill' Campbell). Campbell wrote: 'I am afraid the H.B. Co.'s line to the Indians was furs and more furs, and very little enlightment on any other subject.' Campbell married the daughter of David Munroe in 1891. He described his wedding at Oxford House as 'excelled in splendor by the marriage of the Marquess of Lorne to Princess Louise. Princes and Princesses of the great Saulteaux Nation from the surrounding lakes and rivers attended.' Campbell died at Norway House, Manitoba in 1948.

Jack Fiddler (He Who Stands In The Southern Sky): This son of Porcupine Standing Sideways was born in the 1820 decade. While he was known to his people as, He Who Stands In The Southern Sky, the HBC fur traders called him, Mesnawenne, meaning, Fancy Man. Records contain several variations of spelling for this name: Mesnawethins, Mesnawnnie, Maisinawninie, Masenawineno and Masenawine. The first reference to him being called Jack Fiddler comes in 1887 at Island Lake. The trial records indicate that a clan leader had much authority over his followers. His word was The Word. After 1902, when he last came to Island Lake to trade, his sons Robert and Adam assumed much of the leadership for the Sucker clan. He reported, while under his arrest at Norway House, that he had confronted and killed 14 windigos during his long life. He strangled himself on October 1, 1907 at Norway House, Manitoba.

William MacKay: William MacKay was an HBC postmaster at Windy Lake, Island Lake, Big Trout Lake and Berens River between the years 1833-1871. He was the son of the infamous Northwest Company – Hudson's Bay Company fur trader, Donald 'mad' MacKay and a daughter of James Sutherland. He was born in 1793 in the northwest but went to Scotland in 1811, where he lived in the Parish of Clyne, Sutherland County with his father until 1816 when he joined the HBC. He was described by a superior as 'being quite "au lait" in all matters.... Such as Sled and Snow Shoe making, winter voyaging, and above all his Adroitness, in walking in the woods.' Indeed, in the winter of 1830 he walked some 710 miles between January 17th and February 3rd, 'while the thermometers seldom rose above 30° and five or six days during that period the Mercury was Solid.' MacKay retired in 1871 and died in 1887 at 94 years of age. He was buried in St. Andrew's Cemetery, Winnipeg, Manitoba.

Reverend Edward Paupanakiss: Born 1840, Norway House, Manitoba. He was the son of a shaman but became educated under the tutelage of the Reverend James Evans. While in the service of the Hudson's Bay Company, he was converted to Christianity in 1873. He was a religious leader at Nelson House from 1874-1880. Later, he was posted to Oxford House and from this post, he visited Island Lake. William 'Big Bill' Campbell described him as: 'A real gentleman and the best Missionary that ever had come amongst the natives.' Paupanakiss died at Norway House on July 26, 1911.

Reverend John Semmens: Born Perron Downs, Cornwall, England on January 9, 1850. Raised at Bruce Mines, Ontario. Graduated from Victoria College, Toronto. Went to Norway House on Lake Winnipeg in 1872 as a Methodist missionary and held posts at Norway House, Cross Lake, Nelson House and Berens River, Manitoba. In 1895 he was selected to organize an Industrial School at Brandon, Manitoba for native children. In 1901 he joined the Department of Indian Affairs. He was the Treaty Commissioner for Adhesions to Treaty Number Five in 1909-10. His book, *Mission Life in the Northwest* contains strong condemnations of native spiritualism ('the land of paganism and spiritual death') and of Hudson's Bay recruits ('strong as oxen, ignorant as mules'). He died in Winnipeg in February, 1921.

Commissioner Aylesworth Bowen Perry: Born, Napanee, Ontario, 1860. He was the Commissioner of the North West and Royal Canadian Mounted Police from 1900-1922. His papers contain no references to the arrest of Jack and Joseph Fiddler so it is unlikely he regarded this affair as no more than an incident in his duties. He died in Ottawa in 1956.

Sitting In The Sky (Papamekesickquap): Historical records (HBC B.239/2/10) suggest he was the eldest son of Long Legs, a leading hunter in the Upper Severn in the first half of the 19th century. Sitting In The Sky was the leader of the 'Little' Crane clan from Cliff Dweller Lake by the 1870s. Campbell described him as 'a very intelligent man.' His clan were not above encountering Windigo. In 1892, when the Cranes 'gathered together in the spring, a strange Indian visited their camp at nights stealing from the stages, the band pronounced him a Weetigo and wanted to shoot him.' His importance as a shaman among his clan is implied in 1892 when he is reported unwell, and the HBC fur trader at Island suspected this would 'affect the hunts of the whole band as he looked after them.' He died in 1907 at an advanced age.

Reverend Frederick George Stevens: Born October 9, 1869 near Markdale, Ontario. In 1891, he became a devout Christian and he wrote that 'God was able to speak to me. Soon, gently and by degrees He impressed upon me that He wanted me to prepare for work among the Indians.' In 1897, he was posted as a Methodist missionary to Oxford House, Manitoba. In the winter of 1899, he was the first missionary to visit the Sucker, Pelican and Crane clans in the headwaters of the Severn River. (His wife, Frances Pickell, was the subject of a book – 'Frances and The Crees' by Nan Shipley – concerning her life at several northern missions.) Stevens was forced to leave Oxford House in 1902, after he reported the Sandy Lake starvations. But, in 1907, he went to Fisher River, Manitoba. From there, he made trips to Caribou Lake in 1917-18-19. In 1920, his travels were stopped by the Manitoba Conference. He did not return to Caribou and Sandy Lake until 1940 when he went on pension. The Stevens Memorial United Church in Fisher River was dedicated to him for his service there from 1907-1940.

He was often at odds with his superiors in the Methodist and United Church over his concern for native folk. Superiors described him as a 'trying person' and 'a hard man to manage.' His dedication to Adam Fiddler and the clan folk at Sandy Lake, however, is the primary reason the United Church exists there, today.

Stevens was a master of the Cree language and translated hundreds of hymns, many of which he published in a Cree primer called 'The Spiritual Light.' He died in August, 1946 at Norway House, Manitoba. He was the last of a notable group of Methodist missionaries who began to bring Christianity to native people a century earlier.

FOOTNOTES

1. Rae, Edward. 'On Thompson Quill and Jack Fiddler,' page 19.
2. Campbell, William 'Big Bill,' 'Narrative of William Campbell,' Unpublished manuscript, Thunder Bay, Confederation College, page 19.
3. Ibid., page 35-36.
4. HBC B/93a/10, Island Lake Post Journal, 1891, William Campbell.
5. Ibid.
6. Ibid.
7. *Manitoba Free Press*, 'Defends Indian Custom,' Letter to Editor by J. K. McDonald, October 16, 1907.
8. HBC B/93a/11, Island Lake Post Journal, Robert Whiteway.
9. Ibid.
10. Stevens, F.D. 'Autobiography of Reverend Frederick G. Stevens,' Unpublished manuscript, Winnipeg, University of Winnipeg, page 23.
11. Public Archives of Canada, R.G. 10 Volume 4053.
12. Campbell, William 'Big Bill,' 'Narrative of William Campbell,' page 43.
13. Public Archives of Canada, R.G. 18 Volume 324.
14. Public Archives of Canada, R.G. 85 Volume 1044.
15. Ibid.
16. Godsell, P.H., 'The Arctic Trader,' Toronto, 1943, page 83.
17. Public Archives of Canada, R.G. 18 Volume 1044.
18. Ibid.
19. *Manitoba Free Press,* 'In Defense of Indian Custom,' Letter to Editor by L. R. McKay, August 31, 1907.
20. *Manitoba Free Press,* 'Defends Indian Custom,' October 16, 1907.
21. Public Archives of Canada, R.G. 18 Volume 347 File 42, Part Two.
22. Ibid.
23. Lousely, J.A., 'Memoirs of Fourteen of Norway House, Manitoba 1907-1917,' Unpublished manuscript, United Church Archives, Winnipeg.

24. Public Archives of Canada, R.G. 18 Volume 345 File 42, Part Two.
25. Ibid.
26. Ibid.
27. Ibid.
28. Ibid.
29. Ibid.
30. Ibid.
31. Ibid.
32. Ibid.
33. Public Archives of Canada, R.G. 13 B15 Volume 92 File 386A.
34. Ibid.
35. Ibid.
36. Public Archives of Canada, R.G. 10 Volume 4009.
37. Ibid.
38. Cunningham, A.H., 'Letter to Dr. Sutherland,' December 7, 1909, United Church Archives, Toronto, Box 7, File 145.
39. Public Archives of Canada, R.G. 13 B15 Volume 92 File 386A.
40. Thomas, A. Vernon, 'Bringing into Treaty The Indians of the Far North,' *Toronto Star,* November 26, 1910.
41. Fiddler, Adam, 'Adam Fiddler's Syllabic Record Book,' Possession of Thomas Fiddler, Sandy Lake, Ontario.
42. Ibid.
43. Report of Commissioners Cain and Awrey Re Adhesion to Treaty No. 9 for year 1930
44. HBC B473/a/4 Caribou (Deer) Lake Post Journal, 1933, William Hendry.
45. Ibid.
46. Ibid., K. C. Roseborough.
47. Fiddler, Chief Thomas, Letter to F.G. Stevens, December 29, 1944, United Church Winnipeg Conference, Sandy Lake File, 1936-47.
48. Public Archives of Canada, R.G. 10 Volume 6902 File 494/28-3.

GLOSSARY

Clan: Native people in the boreal forest north of Lake Superior claim their earliest origins from various creatures; Sucker, Crane, Caribou, Pelican, Sturgeon. Relationship between clan folk is based on these creatures and early fur traders referred to groups of native people by their clan symbol. The clans are large extended family groupings often numbering a hundred or more people. In the upper Severn River district clans were often allied by marriages and travelled together.

Clan Leader: The leadership of clan people with their common ancestry was hereditary. Usually the eldest surviving son in the inheriting family became leader. This leader received his authority from tradition, the size of his family and his ability to communicate with other-than-humans who assisted him in healing, hunting, and defeating evil forces.

Cliff Dwellers: Are a form other-than-humans that live in the cliffs along rivers and lakes. A cliff dweller has no nose, a hairy face and they are said to paddle stone canoes. In the Severn River district they often give their blessings to a shaman's medicine thus making it potent in curing.

Other-Than-Humans: Clan folk perceived through visions and dreams and through the shaking tent the presence of other-than-humans. They are an integral part of reality. Dead relatives recalled through the shaking tent are one form of other-than-humans.

Shaking Tent: A shaman's tent was made of eight or more poles sunk into the ground and tied together then covered with bark or canvas. The tent was not movable to any degree but a shaman inside it caused it to shake anywhere from 6" to 2' by calling other-than-humans inside it for consultation and prophecies. The phenomena of the shaking tent remains unexplained by western science.

Shaman: Usually a clansman of maturity who has extraordinary abilities gained from vision seeking. Shamen in the forest gain their reputations from their ability to heal and ward off evil other-than-humans. Communicative powers through the shaking tent is one of the shaman's finest skills.

Spiritual Protector: An other-than-human who is a guide and assistant for a person in times of dire need. The spiritual protector is gained during fasting and vision seeking.

Wabino: A yearly thanksgiving ceremony held in the spring when the poplar leaves grow to the size of the beavers ear. It is held to celebrate the clans survival of the long winter months. A longhouse structure, the wabinogamick is built to hold this ceremony which may last several days. The leader of this ceremony is usually the clan leader.

Weesakayjac: An ancient other-than-human reality who appears to be the spirit being of humanity, Weesakayjac displays all the benevolence and unpredictability in the behaviour of human beings. Some of the old clansmen in the north say he died when the white men came in the forests.

Windigo: An evil other-than-human which is very powerful and cannibalistic. Windigo represents the ultimate threat to clan folk in that it paralyses its victims, leaving them helpless before the final assault. Children often play a game called 'Windigo'! One person plays the windigo. The other children form a line and run one behind the other. The windigo tags the last one in the line until all are caught.

BIBLIOGRAPHY

TRANSCRIBED INTERVIEWS

Bartlett, Dr. L. C. 'Health Conditions of Native People At The Berens River Mine 1942-1948,' 33 pages.

Dumond, Father Wilfred. 'Dr. Father Joseph Dubeau and Brother Joseph Dussault,' 3 pages.

Fiddler, Chief Thomas. 'Tom Fiddler's Accident and Other Stories,' 15 pages.

——— 'Robert Fiddler and The Clan Leave Deer Lake and Other Stories,' 34 pages

——— 'Berens River Mine, Elias Rae and Adam Fiddler,' 16 pages.

——— 'On Arrival of Roman Catholics at Sandy Lake; and Thomas Loonfoot,' 30 pages.

——— 'On Travelling As A Child and Other Stories,' 20 pages.

——— 'On Robert Fiddler and Berens River Mine,' 23 pages.

——— 'On Wolves and Northern Animals,' 20 pages.

——— 'On Native Games and Recreation,' 29 pages.

——— 'On Jack Fiddler and Other Stories,' 16 pages.

——— 'On Health Service At Sandy Lake 1950,' 16 pages.

——— 'On John Carpenter's Stories from Slate Falls,' 10 pages.

——— 'On The Fiddler Family; Story of Jimmy Kakekugamick,' 9 pages.

Kakagamick, Ateyen. 'Oh Bill Hendry and Alfred Sterling,' 1 page.

Lindokken, Jean. 'Early Years at Deer Lake,' 20 pages.

Lindokken, Oscar. 'On Thompson Quill,' 4 pages.

Linklater, Thomas. 'On James Linklater and a Native Childhood,' 45 pages.

Rae, Edward. 'On Thompson Quill and Jack Fiddler,' 25 pages.

——— 'On Young Lad, Man Always Sitting, Adam Fiddler and Use of Power,' 40 pages.

Mamakeesik, William. 'Starvation At Sandy Lake,' 6 pages.

Stevens, F.W. 'On F.G. Stevens and United Church,' 21
pages.

UNPUBLISHED MANUSCRIPTS

Campbell, William. 'The Narrative of William "Big Bill"
Campbell,' 54 pages. Confederation College, Thunder
Bay.
Lousely, J.A. 'Memoirs of Fourteen Years At Norway
House, Manitoba 1902-1917,' United Church Archives,
Winnipeg.
Low, A.P. 'Severn River Notebooks 1886,' R6 45 Volume
161, Public Archives of Canada.
McEwen, A.E. 'Four Years at Berens River, Manitoba,'
Possession of McEwen Family.
Stevens, Frances E. 'My Experiences Living In A Missions,'
Biographical Files, United Church Archives, Toronto.
Stevens, Frederick G. 'The Autobiography of Reverend F.G.
Stevens,' 83 pages, University of Winnipeg, Winnipeg.
——— 'How The Gospel Came and Stayed At Sandy Lake,'
Handwritten Notebook, 43 pages, Possession of Stevens
Family.
United Church of Canada. 'Sandy Lake United Church
Correspondence 1936-1964,' Manitoba Conference,
Winnipeg.

PUBLISHED WORKS

Bishop, Charles A. *The Northern Ojibway and The Fur
Trade,* Toronto and Montreal 1974.
Godsell, Phillip. *Arctic Trader,* Toronto, 1943.
Hallowell, A. Irving. *Culture and Experience,* Philadelphia
1957.
Haydon, A.L. *The Riders of the Plains,* Edmonton, 1971.
Stevens, James and Carl Ray. *Sacred Legends of The Sandy
Lake Cree,* Toronto, 1971.
Stevens, James and Thomas Fiddler. *Legends From The
Forest,* Penumbra Press, Moonbeam, 1985.

INDEX

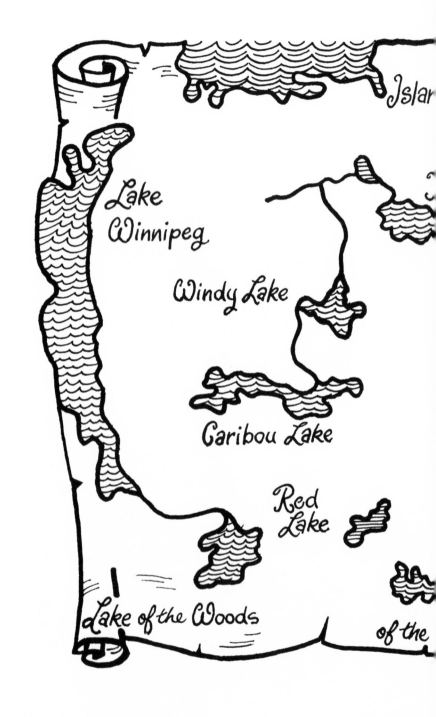

Island

Lake
Winnipeg

Windy Lake

Caribou Lake

Red
Lake

Lake of the Woods

of the

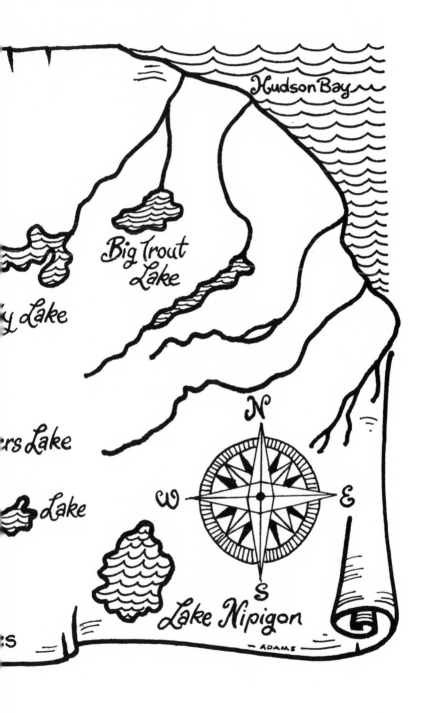